PRAISE FOR WALKING OTHERWARD

Walking Otherward resonates deeply for me. Each reflection begins with a probing question that invites a response from a well-chosen Gospel reading, followed by both inward and Godward reflections of our own. We're then asked to compose an intention that orients prayers of faith to prepare us for life in the world each day. The open-question approach Marc offers makes this prayer book fresh every time the reader returns to it because it grows along with them. Most of all, the book's Christ-centered subtitle is precisely the need of this hour. Those who claim the Christian label will do well to be re-immersed in the Jesus Way while those who don't will discover the path of other-centered, co-suffering love is just what they've longed for, regardless of their faith tradition. I know I will come back to this precious cycle of devotions repeatedly.

— DR. BRADLEY JERSAK / PRINCIPAL, SAINT STEPHEN'S UNIVERSITY

I loved this devotional! It is the first one that helped me delve deeper into my knowledge of God and myself and strengthened my relationship with Him. I would highly recommend this to everyone!

— TRACY ENGLISH / BETA READER

Reading *Walking Otherward*, I couldn't help but call to mind Rainer Rilke's quote: "Be patient toward all that is unsolved in your heart and try to love the questions themselves . . . the point is, to live everything. Live the questions now." Indeed, this is what Marc has invited us into. Through the questions at the end of each devotion and the prayer of intention, the reader is invited on a journey of reflection that welcomes our living.

— FELICIA MURRELL / AUTHOR, SPIRITUAL DIRECTOR

Walking Otherward is an invitation, gently nudging the reader down a path of vulnerability and self-reflection. Its pages offer comfort and a call to grow deeper in one's faith.

— KRISTI MEARS / BETA READER, MENTAL HEALTH THERAPIST

Spirituality doesn't have to be abstract and inaccessible. Marc Schelske invites the reader on a Lenten journey with him, trusting that when we pay attention to scripture and life, we find remarkable ways God is at work. He makes that feel like the most natural thing in the world.

— MANDY SMITH / PASTOR, AUTHOR

Rarely, as a mental health therapist, have I found a devotional that so seamlessly blends spiritual insights with emotional health. With great thought and care for the scriptural text, and a deep love for Jesus, Marc leads us on a journey of self-discovery. Each day the invitation comes to consider the intricacies of our relationship with ourself and God. Marc directs us towards a more other-centered, co-suffering love with the world, as he walks us through the Lenten season. I believe over the forty-day journey you'll find insight and encouragement with this devotional study.

— SHELLEY THORPE / MENTAL HEALTH THERAPIST

Marc's ability in asking such thought provoking questions provided me a process to grow in my love of God. At the end of the forty days, I found myself moving away from a performance fear-based unconscious relationship with God to allowing Him to to see me as beloved no matter what.

— GERALD TAYLOR / BETA READER

In *Walking Otherward*, Marc Alan Schelske guides us on a forty-day journey toward the cross with Jesus, bringing together scripture, reflection, journaling and prayer to invite us to an open-handed, open-hearted exploration of the way of Jesus. These forty days will form you to walk this same path of co-suffering love.

— SUSAN CARSON / AUTHOR, DIRECTOR, ROOTS&BRANCHES NETWORK

I loved this devotional! It is the first one that helped me delve deeper into my knowledge of God and myself and strengthened my relationship with Him. I would highly recommend this to everyone!

— TRACY ENGLISH / BETA READER

The tenacity of *Walking Otherward*'s focus is that Jesus is other-centered and co-suffering and that if I am humble-thoughtful of the ways I need to step aside, release ego, or let go of my familiar and comfortable ways–I can be like Him too. Marc helped me see Jesus better.

— RAYNNA MYERS / BETA READER, AUTHOR

Like looking into a mirror, the questions help me to see new areas of my life in new ways while prompting new questions. I may not always like what I see but it helps me to see what might be in the way of loving others and experiencing the Fruits of God's Spirit . . . When I give up my judgment God can give me curiosity instead . . . when I can give up my comfort, God can give me compassion . . . I have a sneaky feeling that the next time I go through this book, I may discover something new.

— SCOTT GOLPHENEE / BETA READER

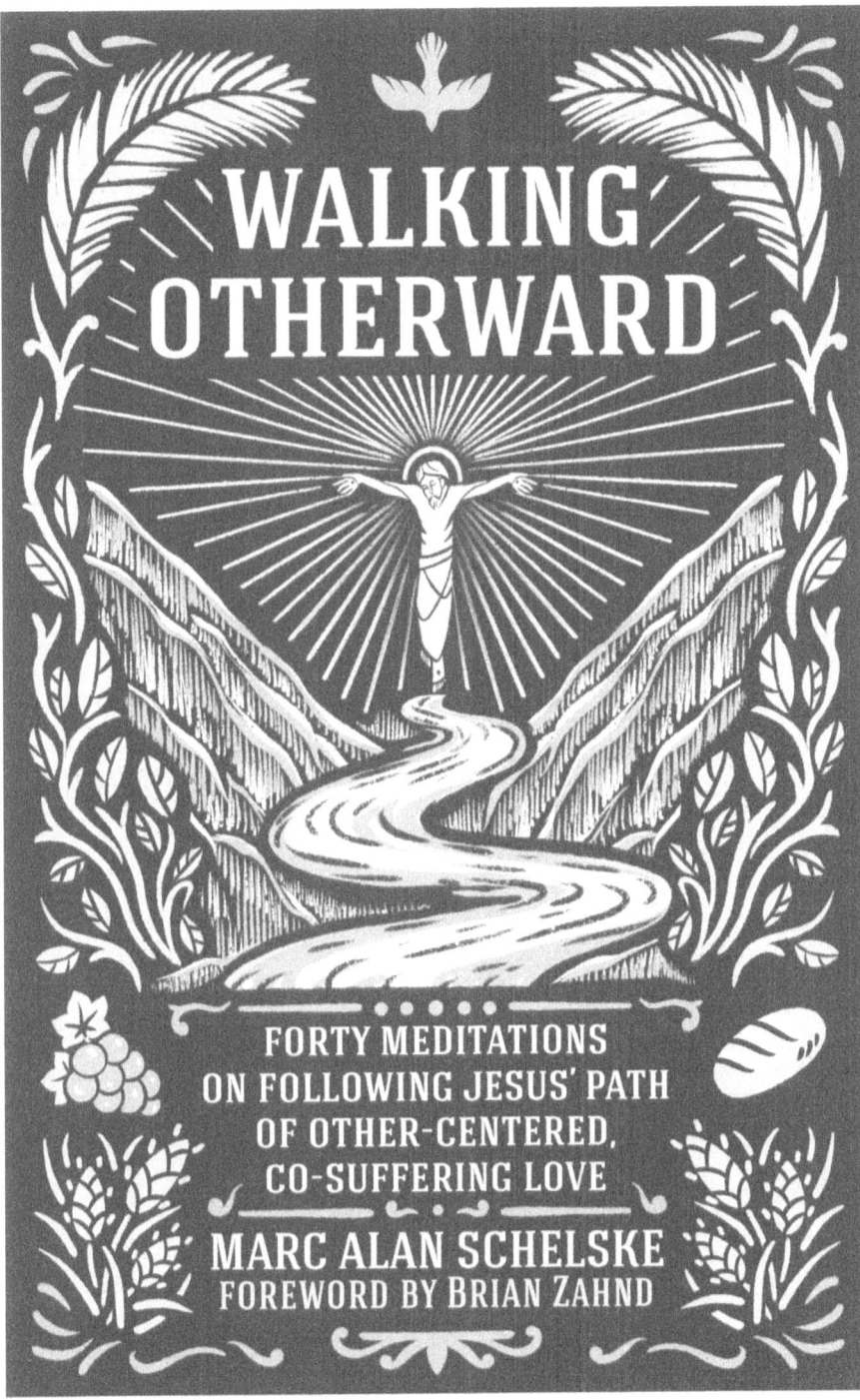

WALKING OTHERWARD

Forty Meditations on Following Jesus' Path of Other-Centered, Co-Suffering Love

MARC ALAN SCHELSKE

Foreword by
BRIAN ZAHND

© 2024 by Marc Alan Schelske. All rights reserved.

Print ISBN 978-0-9886882-4-7

Digital ISBN 978-0-9886882-5-4

Credits: Editor: Leanne Sype; Mental Health Consultant: Shelley Thorpe; Cover Design & Interior Art: Tamara Zabaznoska; Interior Design: 2:ten Creative

Human Made: This book was made by humans. This includes all writing, editing, layout, and art. The only automated tools used in its creation were spellcheck and basic grammar review.

Copyright Notices: No portion of this book may be reproduced, stored in a retrieval system, or transmitted in any form or by any means — electronic, mechanical, photocopy, recording, scanning, or other — except for brief quotations in reviews or articles, without the prior written permission of the publisher. Without limiting the author's and publisher's exclusive rights, any use of this publication to train Generative Artificial Intelligence (also known as Generative Models, Creative AI, Synthetic AI, AI or LLM in any format or model) is expressly prohibited. Submit any use queries to Marc@MarcAlanSchelske.com.

Print License: Purchasers of the ebook edition are licensed to print a single copy for their private use.

All scripture quotations, unless otherwise indicated, are taken from either the New Revised Standard Version Bible (© 2021 National Council of Churches of Christ in the United States of America. Used by permission. All rights reserved worldwide.)

The publisher cannot guarantee the accuracy or functionality of website URLs used in this book beyond the date of publication.

ACKNOWLEDGMENTS

Every moment I am able to step out of the rush of life and all its obligations to write is a gift made possible by those I love —and who love me. Thank you, Christina, Emerson, and Lucas, for making space for me to read, wonder, and write. Thank you, Bridge City family and friends for your encouragement, for engaging my ideas, for putting up with unnecessarily long historical context when we discuss scripture, for sometimes pushing back, and for telling me over and over that my writing work is legitimate and valuable to you.

I want to recognize and thank Brian Zahnd for his role in this book. Brian is a pastor and public theologian thinking carefully about how Christians today, particularly in the modern, Western church, can understand this ancient faith in faithful and constructive ways. This book you hold now grew out of my interaction with his Lent devotional, *The Unvarnished Jesus*.

In 2021, I used his devotional as my guide for Lent, journaling on my sense of who God was inviting me to be. In 2022, I wrote a series of blog posts for Lent that took those same passages and my journaled reflections as the starting point. Conversations around those blog posts and my continued pursuit of understanding the other-centered, co-suffering love of God led to this book. There are several places where I'll quote Brian Zahnd directly. He guided me to a helpful understanding of several passages. While I draw on many sources and my decades of theological study and development, it seems right to say that this book is written in dialogue with his.

I also offer much humble gratitude to Dr. Bradley Jersak, Dr. Peter Fitch, Dr. Walter Thiessen, Dr. Laurens van Esch, Jessica Williams, Dr. LA Henry, Rev. Dr. David Moore, and all the rest of the crew at St. Stephen's University Graduate School of Theology. Your compassionate engagement and sharp thinking was a catalyst for a significant theological shift for me. Many of our conversations found their echo in these pages.

I am so thankful for the many who helped bring this book to life: The most brave and generous of my crew of beta readers whose thoughtful questions made this book better: Karen Bonelli, Brian Borin, Amy Burns, Heather Bacon-Shone, Pauline Evans, Bernard Gildemeister, Scott & Darla Golphenee, Larissa Howell, Lillian Moffitt, Mark Merizan, Raynna Myers and her kids, Becky Peay, Bev Phillips, Kim Puckett, Aaron Smith, Gerry Taylor, Steve Wang, as well as those I only know by first name from our online forum, Benjamin, Jennifer, Liz, and Tracy. Thank you all so much for the good faith and intentional care you put into our discussions.

I am grateful and indebted to a number of folks who added their expertise so this book could be its best self: Shelley Thorpe, who provided a therapeutic review; Leanne Sype, my skilled and gracious editor; Tamara Zabaznoska, who took the content of this book and created the artful cover that I love so much; Susan Carson, who once again kept the book launch on track. Making a book is not a solitary endeavor, and I'm so grateful to have all of you in this with me.

FOREWORD

Virtually all Christians have some affinity for the church calendar, even if they don't realize it. After all, the church calendar is what gives us Christmas and Easter. But the church calendar is far more robust than those two solitary holy days. In reality, the church calendar marks time throughout the year by telling the gospel story. Thus the baptized have two calendars — a secular calendar to coordinate our lives with the rest of the world and a sacred calendar to coordinate our lives with the story of Jesus.

Christmas and Easter are our most important holy days because Incarnation and Resurrection are at the heart of the gospel. Jesus Christ is the Word made flesh who was crucified and raised from the dead for our salvation. But we don't arrive at Christmas and Easter out of nowhere — these glorious feasts are preceded by seasons of preparation. Before the celebration of the birth of Christ (Christmas), we have the season of Advent; and before the celebration of the resurrection of Christ (Easter), we have the season of Lent. (Lent is simply the Old English word for spring.)

However, in the Protestant world, especially among Evangelicals, the church calendar was more or less reduced to the two days of Christmas and Easter. Advent and Lent were seen by many as Catholic innovations and largely ignored. Yet it's more accurate to think of Advent and Lent as early Christian practices preserved in the Catholic church while mostly abandoned in the low church Evangelical world. But all of that has begun to change. Christians from all manner of denominations and non-denominations are rediscovering the wisdom in the ancient calendar. And this is a wonderful thing.

I suspect that the increasing popularity of observing Advent and Lent among non-Catholic Christians in the West is the result of a yearning for two things we desperately lack in our ritual-impoverished secular age: rhythm and roots. The church calendar provides a sense of holy rhythm throughout the year, and the calendar itself is rooted in the ancient practices of the early church. Christianity is a received faith; we don't get to make it up. Along with the creeds and canonical text of the faith, we are also given a calendar. I see it as a hopeful harbinger that the church born in modernity (Protestantism) is at last recognizing the wisdom of our pre-modern sacred calendar.

And so you are about to embark upon a forty-day journey through Lent. This Lenten pilgrimage is a journey through the Gospels with Jesus as he moves resolutely toward the cross. Each reading in this Lenten devotional is preceded by a brief reading from Matthew, Mark, Luke, or John. I encourage you to read these passages, not analytically or critically, but sacramentally. There is a place in academic theology for an analytical and critical reading of the biblical text, but that is not what Lent is about. Lent is an invitation to encounter the text as sacrament.

What do I mean by that? Sacrament (sacred mystery) is a

material means by which we participate in unseen spiritual realities. In the water of baptism, we participate in the death and resurrection of Christ. In the bread and wine of communion, we participate in the body and blood of Christ. And in the pages of holy scripture, we participate in the life of Christ.

As you read and meditate on these Lenten Gospel passages, expect to encounter the unvarnished Jesus who cannot be contained by conventional assumptions and denominational dogmas. Be with Jesus in the sacred text! Allow the living Christ who is sacramentally present in Scripture to surprise, startle, and unsettle you. Allow the living Christ also to comfort, console, and convey peace to you. Don't approach your Lenten journey with preconceived expectations—just be present to Jesus and believe that he will be the living Word you need.

The forty meditations on the Gospel reading in this book come from an experienced and trusted pastor. Marc serves as a faithful guide in helping us find the Christlike paths that are, in his words, "otherward." Indeed, to follow Jesus is to journey outside ourselves and our selfish inclinations toward others in co-suffering love. This is the way of the cross, the way of Jesus. It is also the narrow way that leads to life.

I pray that when you arrive at Easter this year, you will do so as one who has been truly transformed by Jesus along the way. Now, let the adventure begin!

- Brian Zahnd, October 2024

*If you are one of the many who,
whether through intuition or study, are convinced
there must be more to the way of Jesus than what
Christianity in the modern West is offering,
this book is for you.*

You are not wrong.

INTRODUCTION

WELCOME

I am so glad you're here! I continue to be thrilled that folks like you would pick up a book I've written. Even more, I'm amazed that through the ancient magic of words written on a page, you and I can spend some time together. Before we get started, I want to say a little about this book, where I'm coming from, and how you might use it.

WHAT'S THIS BOOK ABOUT?

This is a devotional book. If you grew up in certain Christian communities, you already know what that means. But in case you're not familiar, let me explain. This book comprises forty-one short entries meant to be taken day-by-day. This format invites you to slow down, listen deeply, and sit with the ideas. Slowing down in this way is resistance against our rushed world, where it's so easy to miss what's important. In my spiritual tradition, devotional reading like this is also seen as a way to turn our attention Godward, and that is exactly what I hope to help you do.

Would it serve you to take about six weeks to spend some reflective time thinking about spiritual things, about who you are, and who God is inviting you to be? This book will help you make a space for the kind of reflection that can help you grow up a little bit more. In the Christian tradition, many folks seek out this kind of reflection during the annual season of fasting and reflection called Lent. So, while you can use this book anytime, it has been written expressly with Lent in mind. (If you'd like to understand more about taking forty days for spiritual reflection or what Lent is about, look at Appendix 1: Why 40 Days? Why Lent?)

This devotional follows Jesus as he walks to the cross through a selection of scenes that make up the last months and days of his life. Each daily entry reflects on a particular scene with the primary goal of inviting you to reflect on Jesus' actions, words, and attitude. Jesus' final pilgrimage as he walked toward Jerusalem and his crucifixion has always been deeply important to me. As a Christian pastor, of course, I've had many opportunities to study these passages and preach on them. As someone who longs for a deeper connection to God, these passages have felt like a lost chest containing the treasure I've spent years hunting for. I invite you to take this walk with me and see if these scenes might be as transformative for you as they have been for me.

WHO IS THIS AUTHOR?

I've mentioned that I'm a Christian pastor. Perhaps it would be helpful if I said a little more about that. If you're going to read a book of God-talk, it serves you to know who is doing the talking. Knowing where I'm coming from may mean you decide to set the book down. I don't want to waste your time, after all. It may also mean that knowing the trajectory of my journey, you might feel a little bit safer opening your heart to what is said here.

This year I'll pass thirty years in this work. In all that time, I've learned a good bit about what seems to make the most impact for people who want to go to deeper spiritual places, as well as some of the pitfalls that get in the way. In that time I've also had a profound personal spiritual evolution. I am captivated by Jesus and the life he modeled, taught, and offers to us. While I deeply respect the long journey of church tradition and theology, I also understand that the church has always been made of humans and has often got things wrong. I've learned to hold tightly to Jesus and loosely to almost everything else in my faith tradition.

Today, many people use the word deconstruction to identify the complex and often painful process of moving from a fundamentalist way of seeing faith to something more open. (This word is also used by Christian critics to shame people they see as heretics and apostates.) I can't point to a decisive moment of deconstruction in my life. Rather, my experience is that slowly, since I was a teenager, I've tried to follow Jesus in a deeper and more integrated way. As I've prayed, studied, and practiced, I've found myself guided in a direction that seems more generous and loving. Others might call it progressive or even liberal. Now and then, on social media, I have the strange experience of having folks in my extended Christian family telling me that I'm not a real Christian because of some view I share or some question I ask! Oh well. I will leave the final determination up to Jesus.

With this book and everything I write, I am exploring Christian spirituality in a way that opens up possibilities. I want to broaden the theological conversation for folks whose primary spiritual imagination has been shaped by fundamentalism. I also want to offer a hand to those who have been burned by institutional religion but who are still compelled by Jesus. My vision of the way of Jesus has shifted radically since I was a pastor's kid in the eighties in the U.S. Midwest, shaped as I was by fundamentalism. The other-centered, co-suffering way of Jesus is so much better than what I was handed. The more I walk toward others in a posture of humility and grace, the more I find God's presence. I think you'll find that true, as well.

I think that's enough for you to decide if you want to move forward. If you don't, feel free to set the book down. If this sounds like something that won't work for you, please return the book to wherever you bought it, or if that's not possible, contact me directly at Marc@MarcAlanSchelske, and I'll happily refund your purchase price.

GETTING THE MOST OUT OF THIS BOOK

Moving onward? In that case, I'd like to share a few things with you so you can get the most out of this experience.

Of course, this is your book now, which means you can use it however you like. However you use it, I hope and pray it will enrich and encourage you. It might, however, interest you to know that this devotional has been written to be compatible with the process laid out in another book of mine, *Journaling for Spiritual Growth.** That little book provides a guide that will, over the course of six weeks, help you build a sustainable journaling practice for your own emotional and spiritual growth. If you'd like to learn that process, start there.

---

* You can learn more about this book and even find a copy here: https://marcalanschelske.com/journaling-for-spiritual-growth/

In week four, you'll be encouraged to pick a devotional to accompany your journaling. Well, the book you're holding now is a great option since I designed it to work with the journaling process I teach. If you'd rather just get started without having to read a whole separate book (understandable!) I'll lay out a brief orientation here. This will be more than enough for you to move forward. At some point, if you're interested in the reasoning behind this process, you can always read *Journaling for Spiritual Growth* then.

This devotional book is laid out with 41 entries. If you're using it for Lent, you'll begin on Ash Wednesday. Then you'll have enough entries to read one each day through Easter Sunday, taking one day a week off. If you're using it at another time, just proceed day by day, taking entries as you're ready to move on.

One important note: I've found more success maintaining a daily practice when I build in the expectation that I'll take a couple of days off each week. This makes room for life to happen and takes the teeth out of perfectionistic frustration when you miss a day. Days get missed. That's normal. Any spiritual practice that can't accommodate your real life isn't one you'll stick with.

Each day's entry includes the same elements:

- A title that poses a question about your attitude and orientation toward life. The title matters. It primes you for the direction we're headed.
- A scripture reference.
- My short reflection on that scripture.
- Two questions to serve as a jumping-off point for your own reflection.
- A prayer prompt.

Depending on how deeply you engage the questions and prayer prompt, each day's entry will likely take fifteen to thirty minutes.

I recommend that you start your time of reflection with silence. If you are new to sitting in silence, it will be hard! Some people can only handle a minute or so. Most of our lives don't give us much time for silence. But there are definitely ways, even in a very busy life, to incorporate silence.*

Once you've taken a moment to breathe slowly and quiet your thoughts, proceed with the material. Of course, you can read the reflection and think about the questions in your mind, but my experience is that writing these thoughts and prayers down is far more effective for most people. I get into the reasons for this in *Journaling for Spiritual Growth*. Here, I'll simply say that I expect your season of spiritual focus will be more effective if you journal your reflections and prayer prompted by this devotional. Further, in the very last entry, you'll be invited to reflect on your thoughts and prayers along the way, so keeping them in a journal will help you do this.

The scriptures are drawn from the final season of Jesus' life as presented in the four canonical Gospels and proceed roughly chronologically. To save space, only the scripture references are listed, rather than printing the passage in full. That means you'll need to look up those verses in a Bible, a Bible app, or on a website.

These scriptures were chosen, and the reflections written, to invite you to think about your own attitude and

---

* Practicing a few minutes of silence can be quite hard for those of us accustomed to busy, noisy living. In *Journaling for Spiritual Growth*, I offer a number of simple practices you can try, and offer a list of great resources, including other books that can help you learn to practice silence in an intentional way. If silence is new to you as a spiritual practice, I invite you to take some time to learn more about it.

orientation toward life. If you are already a follower of Jesus, consider this an opportunity to bring your thoughts and attitudes more into alignment with Jesus' example. If you aren't a follower of Jesus, these questions will still be fruitful. Perhaps these reflections will give you a deeper understanding of this person who was so compelling that those who knew him in person testified that in him, they experienced a unique presence of Divinity.

The response section always follows the same pattern: An Inward Reflection, a Godward Reflection, and a Prayer of Intent.

The Inward Reflection will invite you to reflect on the theme of the passage as it relates to your inner life. This question might touch on your emotional reality, spiritual experience, and even your sense of self, including how you see your identity and how you move in the world and interact with others.

The Godward Reflection will invite you to reflect on what this passage might show you about the character of God. If the questions make you feel uncomfortable, it might be interesting to reflect on why you are having that reaction. If you find that you simply don't connect with one of these questions, feel free to substitute your own.

Closing your response time is **the Prayer of Intention**. You'll be invited to write a prayer, taking whatever has emerged through the day's entry and investing it with intention. The goal of all spiritual practices is not just to learn something but to change as a person. (Really, the entire response section is prayer if you engage it with an open-hearted intention that the Spirit is present and listening.) The Prayer of Intention is designed to move you out of thinking abstractly so you can declare your intention for the day regarding who you are becoming and, perhaps, who you think God is inviting you to be.

Again, if the questions and prayer prompt don't connect with you, just focus on whatever the reading brought to mind. Trust the guidance of the Spirit present with you. If the reflection questions I've written don't connect with you, a quick jumpstart you could use would be to start writing for each section with the following sentence starters:

- God, I hear ...
- God, you are ...
- God, I commit to ...

As you proceed day by day, give yourself space to miss a day here and there; otherwise, you're not likely to make it.* Once you've worked through all the entries, allow yourself a few weeks to let the insights from this experience percolate. Go back and review what you've written. Notice what prayers seemed the most compelling. Notice the themes that resonated. Trust that God is at work in your deep places, bringing you more and more into alignment with the image of Jesus.

Now, a word on the direction of my reflections. This might be important if you are a Christian coming to this book with existing strong theological opinions. You have very likely already heard other interpretations of these passages. Because modern Christianity tends to read the Bible hunting for the

---

* Having said that, if your intention is to make it through, then keep coming back. Spiritual practices have more impact when we are consistent with them. As Jennifer, one of my beta readers said, a good principle is "never miss twice." The point is not the number of days, but that you keep momentum. No judgment if you miss, just wisdom if you intend to build a spiritual practice.

One True Meaning of the text (which is a much different way of reading scripture than Christians in the past), you may find the angle I take on some passages quite different from what you've heard.* These reflections emerged from my own devotional study of the passage, focusing on how this passage might shape my attitude as a follower of Jesus. That's what I'm offering to you. Second, you are under no obligation to accept my viewpoint and interpretation. I hope the reading I offer will invite you to consider your attitude and the way you handle scripture. I trust that, like the Bereans who so impressed Paul,† you will adopt what you find to be fruitful and true and discard the rest.

If the passage or my take on a passage brings up any discomfort, please consider the possibility that this discomfort might be a useful tool for your journey. The underlying perspective that shapes the reflections in this book is that the decisive quality of God's nature is other-centered, co-suffering love. It seems to me that following Jesus means following this same path. But this path is challenging, particularly because it contradicts many cultural and even theological preconceptions many of us have. Don't dismiss discomfort and cognitive dissonance as ways to see God more clearly. When we read scripture that doesn't align with our sense of who God is, that is an invitation to further reflection.

St. Augustine addressed this problem when he wrote about making sense of difficult passages of scripture:

---

* If my statement that Christians in the past read scripture differently than we often do today caught your attention, and you'd like to learn more about what I mean, a great starting point is Dr. Bradley Jersak's excellent book, *A More Christlike Word*. https://amzn.to/4eBV271

† Acts 17:10-11.

In regard to figurative expressions, a rule such as the following will be observed, to carefully turn over in our minds and meditate upon what we read till an interpretation be found that tends to establish the reign of love.*

Keep mulling it over, he says, until we get to a reading that leads us to love. That is what we are here seeking.

It means a lot to me that you would share some of your precious time with me. It's my hope and prayer that as you take the time to reflect on these things, you will find your way to a deeper and wider experience of the life God's given you. If you have questions or want to share what's happening for you as you read, I'd love to hear. You can email me at Marc@MarcAlanSchelske.com.

- MAS, June 2024

---

* This is from *On Christian Doctrine*, Book 3, Chapter 15, Verse 23.

*By your holy incarnation and birth,
make us love our humanity!*

*By your poverty and servanthood,
teach us to be lowly in this world!*

*By your powerlessness and weakness,
Strengthen our weakness!* *

---

* Niklaus Ludwig von Zizendorf, Erb, *Pietists*, 297.

DAY 1: WHERE IS MY MIND SET?

Mark 8:27-33*

REFLECTION

SOMETIME IN FEBRUARY, when it is cold and often dreary, some Christians show up to work or school with a gray smudge on their foreheads. If you pulled them aside to let them know so they could clean themselves up without embarrassment, you'd probably be shocked to learn it was on

---

* If you're new to reading scripture, then you'll need to know how a scripture reference works. That's what this is! Don't feel embarrassed. Everyone has to learn this at some point. A scripture reference, also called a citation, is just an address. The sequence of the address is Book, Chapter, Verse. Today's passage is Mark 8:27-33. This tells you to go to Mark's Gospel. That's the second book in the New Testament. The "8" tells you to open to the 8th chapter of Mark. The ":27-33" tells you which specific verses to read. So, Mark's Gospel, chapter 8, verses 27 through 33. If you're using a Bible website, like www.BibleGateway.com or an app, you'll be able to enter the reference, and you'll be taken directly there.

purpose! If you didn't grow up with this tradition, undoubtedly, it seems strange.

Forty-six days before the Church celebrates the resurrection on Easter, many Christians head to church for a short mid-week gathering. They leave this Ash Wednesday service wearing the mark of ashes. This might seem an odd practice that feels out of time to some, strangely earthy, even unkempt in contrast to the attention most of us give to our appearance. But that would not be the experience for those who know the beauty of the ashes.

Ash Wednesday marks the beginning of the venerable fast of Lent. Those ashes evoke the ancient words, "For you are dust, and to dust you shall return."* It also offers a humbling medicine when our personal mythology has grown too inflated: Remember where you came from. Remember where you are headed. These two signposts offer guidance for anyone seeking a healthy way of being human. Whether observing Lent or simply beginning a new season of attention to spiritual things, these two signposts will serve you well.

Remember where you came from. Remember where you are headed. You and I are miracles. We are also animated dust. We are spiritual fireworks already falling and fading, dancing bodies slowly being taken by entropy. If we are willing to sit in the vulnerable discomfort of this tension, we have a beautiful opportunity.

At a turning point in Mark's Gospel, Jesus tells his friends that soon those in power are going to kill him. His friends don't receive the news well. After all, Jesus had only just healed a blind man, and people were saying he might be the Messiah. His crowds were growing. Peter, the leader among the disciples, pushed back in a private rebuke to Jesus. I

---

* Genesis 3:19.

imagine Peter telling Jesus he was being too negative. How could Jesus build a following by saying things like that?

Jesus' response is still startling. "Get behind me, Satan!" Jesus then claims Peter's mind is set on "human things" rather than the "things of God." I expect Peter was surprised by this. Maybe even hurt. How could Peter's desire to support Jesus' success be bad? Not just a mistake, but something satanic?

Considering the context, I wonder if the "human things" Jesus refers to are our narratives of success. More influence, more money, more power. For a good person, don't these open the opportunities to do more and bigger good things? After all, isn't that what a blessing looks like? More happiness. Bigger accomplishments. More prosperity, in whatever way we imagine it. Surely, these things show that God is at work — at least, some seem to think so.

In this interaction with Peter and throughout his life and teaching, Jesus points in a different direction. He challenges us to set down our instinct of self-protection and desire for elevation. In this interaction, Jesus begins talking about his soon-to-be-experienced cross. Like Jesus, we are encouraged to become cross-bearers. This is a shift of mindset. Trade vengeance for forgiveness. Trade personal security for bearing one another's burdens. Trade heroic individualism for a community of mutual care. Trade the pursuit of more influence, money, and power for the pursuit of more intimacy, generosity, and compassion. Jesus sums this all up by saying that if we want to save our lives, we must lose them first.

The way of Jesus always passes through death. It's natural to want to avoid discomfort. That's human. At the same time, it's a bit weird for followers of the One who walked to the cross to focus their lives on avoiding discomfort. As far as Jesus is concerned, the cross is the only way to life. We lose our lives to find them. We die to live again. These words are not about eternity. Or, at least, not just about eternity.

Over these forty days together,* we will follow Jesus on his long walk toward the cross. Like all long walks, this one offers plenty of time to think. In choosing these scripture passages, I invite you to consider who you are becoming. For many, the name "Christian" has come to mean a particular package of politics, culture, and lifestyle, but that is a misdirection. To follow Jesus means to follow his way — His way of thinking, living, seeing, and interacting with others. This is the way that we see in these gospel texts. The normal human mind is set on security, gaining influence, winning, and making things happen how we want when we want. This is not Jesus' way. Jesus calls us to turn from ourselves, to die to self in service and love. Miraculously, death is the path to resurrection.

Remember where you came from. Remember where you are headed. Ashes to ashes, dust to dust. We are fragile; we will die. But also in the death of self and ego, like seeds planted in the earth, we are born to a new kind of life.

---

* Or 46, if you're following this for Lent, or however long you take to make it through.

INWARD REFLECTION

You are animated dust, simultaneously a miracle and also incredibly vulnerable. How might keeping this in mind impact the way you think about your life?

GODWARD REFLECTION

Peter wanted Jesus to focus on growing influence and power. So when Jesus mentioned his upcoming death, Peter rebuked him, perhaps in a very human attempt to avoid discomfort. In what ways might God be inviting you to pay attention to vulnerability, loss, and death that you'd rather avoid? If you find that you'd rather not answer this question, spend some time reflecting on why that is. Discomfort and avoidance are almost always instructive.

PRAYER OF INTENTION

Each day, I'll ask you to write a short prayer that expresses how you want to act or live in response to the reading and your reflections. I will offer a direction for this prayer, but trust the Spirit at work in you, and if what is arising for you takes you in a different direction, follow that. Considering today's reading and your reflections, write a prayer that expresses who you want to be and how you intend to live this out today.

DAY 2: WHICH WAY AM I CHOOSING?

Luke 4:1-13

REFLECTION

JESUS WAS HEADED toward the cross long before he took that final road to Jerusalem. Immediately after his baptism he headed into the wilderness. There, he experienced forty days of deprivation and three temptations. Jesus' response to the temptations defined the course of his ministry—how he would go about what he would do.

The first temptation was to use his divine power to feed himself. The second was to validate his relationship with God through a spectacle of power. The third was to receive power over all the human kingdoms by paying the low, low cost of submitting to Satan. The New Testament letter to the Hebrews tells us Jesus was tempted "in every way," just like we are.* But aside from the temptation to avoid suffering that

---

* "For we do not have a high priest who is unable to sympathize with our

Jesus faced in the garden prior to the crucifixion, this scene in the wilderness is the only time we explicitly see Jesus facing temptation. That's odd. At first glance, these don't seem to be the everyday struggles we all face.

Jesus' baptism was the beginning of his public ministry. Before this, he was an obscure tradesman. After this, he would become a public figure. During those forty days of testing, Jesus chose his path. How would he go about his work? We often overlook the necessity of this kind of decision. When we set ourselves to some good goal, any means that can get us there seems worth considering. I suspect that's the heart of Jesus' temptations, too. In each case, he set down self-elevating power, relinquishing it as a resource for accomplishing his mission.

Why would Jesus do this? I suspect it is because the way we proceed changes us. Setting goals matters, but how we pursue our goals matters more. The means we choose inexorably shape the outcome. Haven't we all been tempted to shortcut the gentle pacing of love? Will we use whatever power or privilege we have for our own gain or security? Or will we trust God's timing and follow the slow, non-manipulative, non-coercive path of love? We can either live from a place of self-centered, ego-defending ambition or we can take the path that leads down and away from this, the path of other-centered, co-suffering love.*

---

weaknesses, but we have one who in every respect has been tested as we are, yet without sin." Hebrews 4:15, NRSVue.

* This phrase represents what I take to be the heart of Jesus' example and teaching. The Christian church as a whole has not always, or even often, aligned with this path, but this is what the best of Christian spirituality offers. This other-centered, co-suffering posture can be found in the lives of countless (often anonymous) Christians and their churches across time and history—as well as folks who don't even identify as Christians. These faithful followers of Jesus served others at great cost, walked with those in the

Through his wilderness temptations, Jesus choose how he would pursue his goals. With his invitation to follow, Jesus asks us to walk with him on this path.

INWARD REFLECTION

Jesus' three temptations were invitations to pursue his good goals using the shortcut of self-protective and self-elevating power. What shortcuts tempt you away from the path of love? What might you gain by taking the longer, slower path? What would this longer path look like for you?

GODWARD REFLECTION

If Jesus was God, as Christians claim, and if Jesus chose not to use Divine power to achieve his aims, what does that say to you about the nature of God?

PRAYER OF INTENTION

Write a prayer that expresses who you want to be regarding the ends and means of your life and how you intend to live this out today. Be clear — this is not about what you will accomplish or some perfectionistic need to do what you're already doing better. This is an opportunity to express your hopes and intentions as you listen to your sense of how the Spirit might invite you forward. All is grace.

---

margins, and sought to make the world a more just and peaceful place. The co-suffering part comes from the work of Orthodox Archbishop Lazar Puhalo. I *think* I'm the one who added the other-centered part, although that's just stating explicitly what must naturally be part of co-suffering. For theology nerds, this is a more explicit framing of what is often referred to as Kenotic love or Kenosis.

DAY 3: DOES JUDGING IMPEDE MY VISION?

Luke 7:36-50

REFLECTION

FOUR CANONICAL BOOKS recount the life and teachings of Jesus. They don't all tell the same stories. They each have their own emphasis. So, when a particular episode appears in all four books, I take that as a cue to pay close attention.*

All four Gospels recount a particular dinner party, with Jesus as the guest of honor. During the meal, a woman interrupts the proceedings. She had not been invited. She

---

* Each of the four Gospels was written by different people in different communities of Jesus followers living in different regions. While they all tell the story of Jesus, they do so from different viewpoints and with different audiences in mind. Many Biblical scholars believe the Gospels were assembled from oral stories passed around about Jesus. This may be one reason why the different Gospels might tell different stories, or even tell the same stories in different ways. When the same story shows up in all four canonical Gospels, it's likely because it was an important story in the wider Christian community that had wide circulation. This is one of those stories.

broke open a small bottle of aromatic oil and anointed Jesus' feet. In one telling, the woman used her hair like a towel to wipe the oil from Jesus' feet.

Anointing isn't commonplace today, but it was a familiar ritual act in Jesus' time and culture. Anointing marked a person as dedicated to a particular task. For instance, priests and kings were anointed as they entered their roles. Depending on the status of the role, the oil could be costly. Another time anointing was common was in the preparation of a body for burial.

In all four tellings, the woman's intrusion provoked a stern reaction. In the Gospels of Matthew, Mark, and John, someone in the room spoke up, complaining this was an embarrassing and irresponsible waste of money. In Luke's Gospel, the problem wasn't the lavish waste but the woman herself. The host, another influential religious leader, judged this woman sinful and unworthy. It offended him that she was here, at his event, and even worse, that she touched Jesus.

Then Jesus intervened. In Matthew and Mark, he counters the criticism with affirmation, saying that this woman was doing a beautiful thing, especially since the time left for honoring him was running out. In John's Gospel, Jesus specifically receives the anointing as preparation for his death. In Luke's version, Jesus redirects attention by telling the host a parable about who is more likely to love lavishly. The woman was expressing much love because Jesus had rescued her from something dark, offering her deep forgiveness and renewal. In three of the Gospels, Jesus says her act would be remembered as long as his story is told. (Here we are, talking about it!)

When this woman interrupted their important event with her unexpected behavior, most people in the room missed what was really happening. Something impeded their vision.

In all four versions of the story, people couldn't see the woman's act of love because it violated their expectations. In Luke, the critic spoke moral judgment. Based on his assessment, he thought the woman had no right to be near Jesus. His moral condemnation impeded his vision.

In Matthew, Mark, and John, however, the critics have a point. This was an extravagant purchase. In keeping with Jesus' teaching, this money could have been used to care for those in need. These nay-sayers were right. Even so — perhaps because of their certainty — judgment impeded their vision.* One of the most severe impediments to seeing the dignity of others arises when we start measuring the authenticity, morality, and orthodoxy of their pursuit of God.

My extended Christian family of faith seems to have majored in this ability over the centuries. We've invested so much time and energy into deciding who is pursuing God correctly and which spiritual practices are acceptable. Sometimes, in our judgment, we're wrong. We measure the wrong things and exclude people because of it. Other times, we're right. We can quote chapter and verse confidently. And yet, whether we are right or wrong when our focus is on measuring and weighing the spiritual experience of others, we are not walking the way of love. When we dehumanize others, we will always miss the presence of God.

---

* In John's Gospel, Judas the Betrayer is the main critic. While he was right about how the money could have been used for the poor, secretly he wanted to get his hands on the money for his own use. He's not the first or last case of a person using morality and religion as a cover for their own greed.

INWARD REFLECTION

Reflect on a time when you misjudged someone's intentions or when being judgmental fogged your vision of others. How did this experience impact you?

GODWARD REFLECTION

What does Jesus' response in this story tell you about God's nature and how God sees you?

PRAYER OF INTENTION

In response to these thoughts, write a prayer expressing the role of judgmentalism in your life (whether as the one judged or the one judging) and who you want to be going forward.

DAY 4: DO MY EXPECTATIONS OBSCURE THE DIVINE?

Luke 9:28-36

REFLECTION

ONE DAY, Jesus took Peter, James, and John on a mountain hike. At the summit, they shared a mountain-top experience. They were hiking, and then Jesus started glowing bright as the sun. Two of the most famous historical figures of Jewish history, Moses and Elijah, appeared and started chatting with him. Overwhelmed, Peter suggested they "build shelters"* for Jesus and his eminent guests. Just then, a cloud settled over everything, and the Divine voice was heard saying, "This is my son, the beloved one. Listen to him."

The disciples didn't understand this experience as it was happening. They only began to make sense of it after the

---

* The Greek word translated shelter is σκηνή or *skēnē*. Literally this means tent, but it's also the word used to refer to the Tabernacle in the Exodus story. It might be fair to think of Peter suggesting that they put up something that is part shelter, part shrine.

resurrection. When Jesus spoke about his upcoming torture and death, they thought he was confused or speaking in parables. Peter chastised him for saying something so dark. Two other disciples were so confident about how the trip to Jerusalem would turn out that they pulled Jesus aside to ask for the most prominent cabinet positions in his new government. None of them really heard what Jesus had been telling them.

Moses and Elijah's appearance at the summit wasn't just a reunion with two famous historical figures. Moses was the law-giver; Elijah, the quintessential Hebrew prophet. The law and the prophets. By the time of Jesus, that phrase had become a stand-in for scripture and, thus, for God's revelation. Jesus was in high company on that mountain. Even so, when the cloud disappeared, the only one left visible was Jesus. What words echoed in the ears of the disciples?

"Listen to him." Listen to him alone. The disciples could not hear Jesus clearly, though. Their ears were filled with the noisy anticipation of their preconceptions. They thought they knew what God was up to. What they wanted from Jesus made it impossible for them to hear him.

Their well-meaning misunderstanding stands as warning and invitation to those of us who claim to follow the way of Jesus. Are our preconceptions getting in the way of an encounter with Jesus? What other voices occupy our attention? Are there influences, commitments, or expectations we're tempted to enshrine alongside Jesus, allowing them an equal force in our lives? Are we so committed to our ideas about economics, social structure, or politics that we can only hear Jesus in ways that justify and support those commitments? Are we so wrapped up in an identity story — about self, family, or nation — that we can't clearly hear Jesus?

Attachments like these are particularly powerful when they are about God. Theology can be a wonderful exploration of the nature of God and what that means for our lives. It can also quickly become rigid dogma, preventing us from seeing when God moves in ways we don't expect. Our preconceptions of how the Spirit will work can be the very thing that makes us confident the Spirit isn't at work in our lives or churches — especially if one of our expectations is that the Spirit's presence will feel different or dramatic. The Spirit is often so gentle, committed to the long, slow work of transforming love. It's often hard to see the garden grow while it's growing.

Those of us familiar with the whole narrative arc of the Gospels can read passages like this with the advantage of retrospection. How can the disciples be so clueless, we might wonder. But that thinking is a trap! These were ordinary people, caught up in the perspectives and expectations they held, exactly like we are. That's the trouble with these preconceptions and attachments. When we're in the middle of them, we cannot see how much we are not seeing. If it happened to the people who got to walk with Jesus in person, it could happen to us, too.

INWARD REFLECTION

What are some expectations you currently have of God? (A challenging question for some! But if you allow yourself to be honest, I bet some expectations will surface. These expectations could be positive and helpful or negative and unhelpful.) How might these expectations impact your ability to see or experience Jesus at work in your life?

GODWARD REFLECTION

In the cloud, the Divine voice spoke to Jesus' friends, saying, "Listen to him!" What might this injunction mean for you today in your life? Are there expectations you hold that might get in the way of listening to Jesus, whatever that means for you? Do you have practices that help you listen for the Spirit?

PRAYER OF INTENTION

In this passage, God tells the disciples to listen to Jesus. Your prayer of intention today might be focused on any preconceptions that limit your ability to listen to Jesus, or perhaps you might focus on the "noise" that seems to obscure your hearing.

DAY 5: CAN I TRUST GOD WITH MY UNBELIEF?

Mark 9:17-29

REFLECTION

WHILE JESUS WAS up on the mountaintop with Peter, James, and John, something else was happening below. A man brought his epileptic son to see Jesus, hoping for a cure, but Jesus was away. The waiting disciples tried their hand at healing but weren't successful. When Jesus returned, the desperate father asked Jesus for healing.

Jesus' reply is confounding. "All things can be done for the one who believes."* This response almost makes faith seem like a magical power you could spend on mighty feats. Certainly, remarkable things happen in scripture credited to faith, but history and personal experience suggest that life doesn't usually work this way. Terrible things still happen to faithful people. Desperate prayers seem to go unanswered.

---

* Mark 9:23, NRSVue.

God rarely intervenes, certainly not with the consistency necessary to construct a precise and predictive theology of prayer.

On the other hand, I have a few odd experiences that seem miraculous. I have friends with even weirder stories than mine, including a couple who have experienced miraculous healing. To think our scientific vision sees everything perfectly is arrogant. So, when Jesus says, "All things can be done for the one who believes," I find myself caught in an uncomfortable and seemingly unresolvable tension. Does Jesus mean God's intervention depends on the intensity or quality of our belief? From the response of the frantic father, it seems that's what he heard. His cry is so human, so familiar to me: "I believe; help my unbelief."

Because I know the pain within that cry, Jesus' response intrigues me. He didn't chastise the man for his doubt or uncertainty. He didn't ask this father to prove his faith. Jesus didn't tell the man to pray harder or to use better words. Nothing in Jesus' response indicates the level or quality of belief matters at all. Jesus simply heals the son.

Moments before, Jesus had laid out what sounded like criteria for God's intervention. This father couldn't claim to be living up to that standard, but he didn't leave. He didn't give up. Instead, he entrusted his imperfect experience to Jesus. I get it. I can say, "Yes, I believe." There's a part of me that hopes and trusts. At the same time, I can truthfully say, "I don't believe." I've been hurt. I've got my own archive of unanswered prayers. And I can see a whole world of unjust suffering around me. So, I believe, but also I don't. Maybe the father's significant act of faith was trusting that Jesus would accept his insufficient faith.

In modern usage, the words faith and belief seem abstract. In most modern usage, a belief is an idea one holds to be true, although usually with a connotation that the idea isn't verifiable. (We don't teach elementary school kids "math beliefs." We teach them math facts.) We also use the word belief to encompass concepts of morality and spirituality, as well as philosophical ideas and systems. In some circles, faith refers to the complete collection of religious ideas and practices one holds. In other circles, it means a vague spiritualized hope that you buttress with affirmation and intense feelings. None of those definitions seem to have anything to do with what Jesus was talking about.

In the New Testament, the same Greek word, translated as either belief or faith, can also be translated as trust.* Might Jesus be asking for trust? This is a word that takes us out of the fog of abstraction. This isn't about maintaining a certain intensity of ardor. Trust grounds us in the world of relationships. The deeper the relationship, the more experienced the relationship, the greater the trust. At the same time, only the slightest inclination of trust can be enough to start a relationship.

The father's cry seems to be this inclination. "I believe; help me with my unbelief!" He's not demanding. He expresses no certainty. He's not trying to trade intensity of feeling or performative certainty for divine favor. He turns toward Jesus with a fragile hope — and for Jesus, that's enough.

---

* The noun is πίστις or *pistis*. The verb form is πιστόω or *pisteuo*. Both have the dual meaning referring to what you believe intellectually and also what or whom you trust.

INWARD REFLECTION

What does the desperate father's cry, "I believe; help my unbelief," mean to you in the context of your life? Do you relate? Why?

GODWARD REFLECTION

In this story, Jesus responded positively to this father, even when this father couldn't muster complete confidence or faith. What might this suggest about God?

PRAYER OF INTENTION

Write your own version of the "I believe; help my unbelief" prayer as it applies to your life right now.

DAY 6: DO I USE JESUS TO JUSTIFY MY HATE?

Luke 9:52-55

REFLECTION

ONE AFTERNOON, JESUS' disciples asked him to incinerate a village. They were traveling toward Jerusalem, and the route took them through Samaria. The folks who lived there, the Samaritans, were descendants of the people of the Northern Kingdom of Israel who were left in the land when many from Judah were taken into exile by the Babylonian empire. This had happened some six hundred years prior.

Over the generations, they had intermarried with their neighbors. When the exiles returned, the Samaritans weren't particularly welcoming. Starting from that animosity, there was ongoing contention between the Samaritans and the Jews over their shared history. They disagreed over what counted as scripture. They disagreed over the location of the temple. Feelings between them ranged from condescension and dismissal to hatred.

Jesus had sent some disciples ahead to a Samaritan village to make arrangements. The villagers refused to host them. Refusing hospitality in this time and culture was a great offense. Angered, James and John asked Jesus for permission to firebomb the entire village! (Technically, they asked Jesus to call down fire from heaven.)

Here's where things get interesting. Some ancient manuscript variations end the brothers' request in Luke 9:54 by saying, "as Elijah did." These words are not in the best, oldest Greek manuscripts, so they only appear as a footnote in most modern translations. Even so, what does Elijah have to do with this? Well, eight hundred years earlier, the famous prophet got into a dispute with the king of Samaria. When the king sent soldiers to arrest him, Elijah called down fire from heaven and destroyed the troops. He did this twice to two different groups of soldiers and almost did it to a third detachment before agreeing to have a civil conversation!*

Perhaps these three words at the end of the passage in Luke result from some ancient copyist's discomfort. After all, these holy men were just asking Jesus to do something Elijah did before! That's a handy Biblical justification that puts the disciples above reproach. Maybe James and John had this event in mind. They were in Samaria, after all. If they added "as Elijah did," they were supporting their request with an argument from scripture. "See, Jesus! There's precedent. Here's chapter and verse! God took vengeance on people like this!" Jesus rejected their request. The text actually says he rebuked them. That seems pretty serious.

The legacy of quoting scripture to support our desire to win, injure, or dominate others is long indeed. We may even

---

* You can read the whole dramatic story in the Old Testament book of 2nd Kings, chapter 1.

be seeing this dark human tendency in the disciples themselves! Scripture has been used to justify slavery, genocide, invasions, bombings, and every kind of social hierarchy meant to keep certain people in power at the expense of others.

Unlike what you may have heard, the word Biblical is not an affirmation. Within scripture's pages, actions are recorded and opinions expressed that are not good, moral, or loving. There are even acts people attribute to God that simply do not align with the character of God as revealed in Jesus. Even if Elijah could somehow be justified for calling down fire on his enemies, Jesus repudiates it as an option for the disciples and, thus, for his followers ever after.

We who follow Jesus cannot simply use the label Biblical to justify our desire to punish, exclude, or control others. As important as it is, the Bible is not our Lord and Savior—Jesus is. The standard by which we measure our actions is not "Is it Biblical?" but "Is it Christlike?" The other-centered, co-suffering way of Jesus challenges us to hold our doctrine and scripture carefully, in loving ways, letting go of religious vengeance and spiritual manipulation.

INWARD REFLECTION

The temptation to use scripture to provide spiritual justification for our attitudes and actions toward others is strong.* So often, though, this is just us claiming divine warrant for our desires. Has this ever come up in your life? If so, how and why?

GODWARD REFLECTION

What does Jesus' rejection of the disciple's request for vengeance tell you about God?

PRAYER OF INTENTION

Write a prayer in response to these thoughts. If you feel led to turn away from using spiritual justification to harm or control others, let that be your prayer. If you've felt the temptation to choose shortcuts that require coercion or manipulation rather than taking the longer path of other-centered love, let that be your prayer. If you relate to the passage in some other way, pray in alignment with that.

---

* We could have a great discussion about how this passage is actually the meaning of "taking the Lord's name in vain," rather than superficial ideas about swearing.

DAY 7: DO I LIMIT "WHO IS MY NEIGHBOR"?

Luke 10:25-37

REFLECTION

IN YESTERDAY'S READING, a Samaritan village denied Jesus hospitality. His disciples wanted to retaliate by burning the village to the ground. That should tell you a little about the nature of the relationship between the Judean people (like the disciples) and the Samaritans. That should also prepare you to hear the story Jesus tells in today's reading in a clearer light.

The setting was a conversation between Jesus and a professor in Biblical studies.* This expert asked Jesus what was necessary to receive eternal life. In reply, Jesus asked the man for his reading of scripture. Wisely, the man recited the high standard in Leviticus: "You shall love the Lord your God

---

* Well, an "expert in Torah." The Greek word is νομικός or *nomikos*, which translates as lawyer. But this was an expert in religious law and doctrine. If you imagine a college lecturer who teaches scriptural interpretation, you'll be close.

with all your heart, and with all your soul, and with all your strength, and with all your mind; and your neighbor as yourself."*

Jesus concurred, but the scholar wasn't done. The scholar wanted more nuance, so he asked, "Who is my neighbor?" This was not an innocent question. He and Jesus had just agreed the highest standard was to love your neighbor as yourself. This was a matter of eternal life! Being an expert in religious interpretation, he knew where the ambiguous loophole was hidden. Essentially, this man asked Jesus, "Who exactly am I obligated to love?"

Jesus answered this question with a parable: A man finds himself in a dire situation. He's desperate. He'll likely die without help. Three different people pass by. The first two ignore the dying man. They had their reasons. To make matters worse, those first two are a priest and a Levite. Jesus' audience would reasonably expect these men to be on the front lines of caring for those in need.

The third to come along is a Samaritan — just like the folks the disciples wanted to incinerate! With generations of animosity between them, the crowd might have expected the Samaritan in Jesus' story to loot the man's body and leave him for the crows. Instead, he treated the injured man's wounds, transported him to safety, and arranged medical treatment with a blank-check promise to pay all costs.

The parable stung. The wrong person was the hero! In fact, the hero was precisely the kind of person the crowd was liable to exclude from their circle of care. Jesus closed the story by asking: "Which of these three, do you think, was a neighbor to the man who fell into the hands of the robbers?" Notice that the scripture expert couldn't even bring himself

---

* Luke 10:27, NRSVue. The lawyer was quoting Leviticus 19:18.

to say "the Samaritan." Instead, he vaguely named the good neighbor as "the one who showed him mercy."

In this story, Jesus reverses the expert's question, essentially saying, "You're asking 'who is my neighbor' because you want to know who you can leave outside the circle of your love.* Instead, focus your attention on being a neighbor to anyone in need. The circle of love extends to everyone, even those you think don't deserve it. Even people you consider to be enemies!"

Jesus' famous story presents a challenge for those of us who consider ourselves his followers. Do we find ourselves using scripture to limit the scope of our obligation to love? Do we search for ways to be technically obedient to God without actually loving or serving folks we disagree with? Like the questioning religious expert, we get to choose. Will we be the kinds of people who pass by those in need, protected by our justifications? Or will we take the risk to draw near to them, loving in unexpected moments and costly ways?

---

* Heather, one of my beta readers, put it this way: "By asking 'who is my neighbor?' I am actually asking the opposite: 'who is *not* my neighbor?' I'm pretending I care; but actually, I'm asking God to draw a line so I can decide who's in and who's out (of course, I am always in!)."

INWARD REFLECTION

Are there places in your life where you have asked, "Who is my neighbor?" If so, where and why? (Take note that when we ask this question, we are also implicitly asking, "Who is NOT my neighbor?) What about this person or class of people leads you to want to distance yourself from them?

GODWARD REFLECTION

With this story, Jesus expands the definition of neighbor. In some ways, this is an exciting explosion of grace. In other ways, it's hard. What does this story tell you about God?

PRAYER OF INTENTION

Write a prayer of intention around your definition of who you now consider "your neighbor." What kind of "neighbor" is God inviting you to be? How can you extend the circle wider?*

---

* Steve Wang, one of my beta readers, is responsible for this lovely way of expressing what I think is our central response to God's grace.

DAY 8: DO I CHOOSE BUSYNESS OVER PRESENCE?

Luke 10:38-42

REFLECTION

JESUS and his disciples stop in the small town of Bethany to rest at the home of his friends, Mary and Martha. Famously, Martha got caught up in "her many tasks," while Mary did something different. Mary sat listening to her teacher—exactly what the male disciples did. Martha was frustrated, maybe indignant, about Mary's choice and asked Jesus to tell Mary to get to work. Instead, Jesus told Martha that she was "worried and distracted by many things" but that Mary had chosen the only thing that was truly needed. He wouldn't take that away from her.

In sermons and commentaries, Martha gets a lot of criticism. Some say she should have been worshipping rather than working. Others comment that she was so distracted she wasn't learning from Jesus. You could even make a case that Martha wanted to leverage Jesus' authority to make her sister behave. To defang criticism like this, preachers have often turned this passage into a spiritual personality test. In this view, there are people in the church who are contemplative and others who are task-oriented, people with gifts for worship, and others with gifts for service. Are you a Martha or a Mary? The church needs both! Being a task-oriented person myself, I related to this angle. After all, without the Marthas of the world, the Marys would never eat or have clean laundry!

But the scripture on its face doesn't seem to go there. The text admonishes Martha for being caught up and distracted by her work and affirms Mary's choice to do the one thing that is needful. The correction offered to Martha, and the affirmation of Mary are placed in the mouth of Jesus! So, if this passage feels pointed, perhaps we need to sit with that.

Reflecting on my discomfort with this story, I noticed that one of my assumptions about the scene did not come from the passage. I always thought Martha was occupied with hospitality, preparing food for her guests. This would be both expected and necessary. It would also be work that could be considered an act of service. But this is an assumption. In the text, the nature of Martha's business is not named! Luke simply says, "Martha was distracted by her many tasks." When she complains, she says, "My sister has left me to do all the work by myself." Jesus replies, "You are worried and distracted by many things." Whatever Martha is doing, she thinks of it as "all the work." She thinks it's necessary and needs to happen right now! In her assessment, this unidentified work is more important than taking the opportunity to sit with Jesus (who, it's perhaps worth remembering, will only be in her home for a short time).

Perhaps this isn't a story about different gifts or ensuring we don't let service get in the way of worship. It might not be about the classic tension between active service and spiritual contemplation. I suspect our desire to tip the scale back toward Martha is less about her and more about avoiding the discomfort of being chastened by Jesus. All of us, I suspect, know what it's like to be so distracted and preoccupied that we can't be spiritually present. We've been there; maybe we are there now. To hear Jesus say plainly that being spiritually present is the one thing that matters, well . . . that hurts a bit.

We live in a society that honors accomplishment. Performance is the highest measure of merit. Any task or time slot that doesn't provide value is considered wasted time or maybe a luxury available to those who've finished their chores. I am fully a child of this culture, painfully aware of whether I'm getting things done at any moment. For me and those like me, this passage raises uncomfortable questions.

Am I so caught up in my necessary tasks that I can't be present? Does my need to prove my value through performance mean my unfinished tasks cause me anxiety? Am I driven to work? In my obligation to this never-ending list of tasks, do I feel bitterness toward others who seem free from this kind of driving obligation? Do I consider them lazy, unmotivated, or irresponsible? Is my own internal taskmaster undermining my relationship with those around me? Since the Spirit moves in and through relationships, wouldn't this also impede my ability to be present to the Spirit?

Jesus doesn't chastise Martha for being responsible, for being the kind of person who keeps things orderly, or for getting things done. He observes that she is "worried and distracted." He points out that this internal discomfort is keeping her from choosing the one thing that is most needed in the present moment. It may be hard to hear, but busyness and accomplishment are not the path to peace or a sense of God's presence.

INWARD REFLECTION

What are your biggest internal or personal obstacles to being fully present?

GODWARD REFLECTION

Set aside any sense of judgment or condemnation in Jesus' words. Assume he's speaking from understanding and love. With that in mind, what might this interaction say about God and God's desire for you?

PRAYER OF INTENTION

Write a prayer of intention around matters of distraction in your life that keep you from being present.

DAY 9: AM I TOO FAR GONE FOR GOD?

John 11:1-44

REFLECTION

THE GOSPELS RECORD several actions on Jesus' part that are miraculous. In the Gospel of John, however, these acts are not called miracles. They are called signs. That's an interesting choice of words. Miracles are supernatural events. The point of a miracle is that it breaks natural law. Signs, on the other hand, aren't about the spectacle. They exist to point toward something beyond themselves. Signs tell us where to go or where to look, drawing our attention to something we might otherwise not have seen. For John, then, it seems the significance of the miracle wasn't the miracle itself but what it said about who Jesus was. Keep that in mind.

One day, news reached Jesus that Lazarus, a dear friend, was sick. Jesus told his disciples it was time to return to Judea. The disciples hesitated; they were afraid. The leaders in Jerusalem weren't fans of Jesus. The disciples also didn't understand Jesus' urgency. If Lazarus was ill, he would likely recover. Why should Jesus endanger himself? The disciples still envisioned a future where Jesus would lead the people to overthrow their Roman occupiers. Jesus' death did not figure into that vision!

Arriving, they discovered Lazarus had already been in the tomb for four days! Some of the folks grieving were especially upset because they knew Jesus had healed very sick people. If Jesus had only arrived earlier, he could have saved Lazarus, but Jesus was too late. Death won.

Some things seem so clearly beyond God's reach. Some situations really are hopeless. Four days in the tomb is unequivocal. Yet, Jesus headed to the graveyard. He had the people there roll away the stone blocking the tomb entrance. Jesus prayed. He called out. And then Lazarus — the same one recently deceased — walked into the light.

Lazarus' resurrection was the final straw for the power holders in Jerusalem. It gave Jesus too much influence. That miracle sealed his fate. Supporting Jesus' death warrant, the High Priest said, "You do not understand that it is better for you to have one man die for the people than to have the whole nation destroyed."* He thought he was saying that executing Jesus would preserve the power structure's status quo. He couldn't know that he was describing all of humanity across time.

Don't get distracted by the miracle, though. Look at the sign! God in Christ brings life where there once was death. Now and forever, there is no place too far for God's reach. There is no "far country" too distant, no line we might cross that we cannot come back from. The ancient Psalm writer knew it: "Where can I go from your Spirit? Where can I flee

---

* John 11:50., NRSVue.

from your presence? If I go up to the heavens, you are there; if I make my bed in the depths, you are there. If I rise on the wings of the dawn, if I settle on the far side of the sea, even there, your right hand will hold me fast."*

In our moment of darkness and death, a voice calls us to walk out into the light.

INWARD REFLECTION

Have you had experiences where it felt like Jesus didn't show up? (Take a deep breath. For some of us, even naming these feelings feels sacrilegious. Trust that God can take it.) Are there places in your life where you feel "too far gone?" What are those experiences, and how have they impacted your life?

GODWARD REFLECTION

If this story is meant to give us insight into the nature of God's character, what might Jesus' attitude, words, and actions here tell you about how God relates to you when you feel "too far gone?"

PRAYER OF INTENTION

Write a prayer acknowledging your experience of Jesus "showing up too late" and what you want to say to God about this.

---

* Psalm 139:7-12, NIV.

DAY 10: DO I SHOW UP TO EVERY ARGUMENT I'M INVITED TO?

Matthew 17:24-27

REFLECTION

IN 1ST CENTURY ISRAEL, civil taxes were paid to the Romans, and religious taxes were paid to the temple. One day, a temple tax officer confronted Peter, asking if Jesus was all paid up. Peter said yes, then went and asked Jesus about it—cue teaching moment. Jesus asked Peter if kings collect taxes from their kids. Of course not. After making this point, Jesus takes a more accommodating stance, telling Peter to pay "so that we do not give offense to them."[*] Then he tells Peter to go fishing, suggesting Peter would find what was needed.

At first, Jesus seems to say that families don't tax each other. Essentially, "You and I, Peter, we're children of God. That means the temple tax doesn't apply to us." But if that's the case, the temple tax applied to no one and shouldn't have

---

[*] Matthew 17:27, NRSVue.

existed to begin with. Was Jesus saying that taxes, in general, are something God's not in favor of? The taxation-is-theft crew would undoubtedly agree. Or, since this is a temple tax, was Jesus only talking about financial support of the religious system? The temple tax then, tithes now, and neither should be paid? Or perhaps tithe is acceptable since it's voluntary? What's the point of this interaction?

Some commentators suggest that Jesus' point about the king's children being excluded from taxes is a low-key claim to divinity. If Jesus were the son of God, then he would not be obligated to pay the temple tax. Jesus covering for Peter would be an example of God's provision. Peter didn't need to worry. Jesus had him covered.

Maybe. What is clear is that Jesus thought the temple tax didn't apply to him and Peter, but (and this is the part that intrigues me most) Jesus also seemed to think this disagreement wasn't worth fighting about. I'm drawn to the phrase, "However, so that we do not give offense to them . . ." We know Jesus didn't mind saying or doing controversial things. It seems Jesus wasn't concerned with this disagreement enough to make a scene over it. He had more important things to focus on.

We live in a culture where being right is paramount. Some of us will argue over nearly anything. (Very Online Christians seem to be some of the worst offenders!) If anyone disagrees, we go into combat mode. Think of the spate of videos where someone is denied service or doesn't get their way and throws a fit because they think their rights are being violated. We seem to be losing the ability to know whether a particular conflict is worth the cost. Getting our way and being right has become part of our identity. Choosing to "not offend" doesn't feel like an option. Some of us think that if we don't hold the line, we'll surrender who we are.

I struggle with this. Sometimes, I must consciously decide not to correct someone I think is wrong. Does it count as a spiritual discipline to not respond to every social media post I disagree with? It should! I'm getting better with practice. (No lack of opportunity.) If Jesus thought the temple tax was wrong, wasn't he morally obligated to protest it? Shouldn't he have said something, maybe given a rousing anti-tax sermon in the Temple court? He could have. People would have supported that movement! But he didn't. He paid his tax and moved on. I can only guess he did this because he had more important things to focus on.

Whatever else this passage might mean, it shows us that not every disagreement is worth a fight. Not every ethical difficulty is solved by protest. Sometimes, you must conserve your time and energy for battles that matter.* (Activists, more than anyone else, need discernment here.) This is by no means a call to avoid conflict. Conflict is necessary—especially when ending oppression and injustice are the focus. But we're not obligated to show up to every argument we're invited to.

---

* My editor Leanne pointed out that determining which battles matter is subjective. A battle I think doesn't matter much might be a battle someone else is willing to die for. She's right. It seems to me that an ethic rooted in other-centered, co-suffering love would require me to ask this question compassionately, and if the battle ahead is one that someone else would die for, I might need to consider how to enter into that in a way that is supportive, that bears the burden along with them.

INWARD REFLECTION

How do you react when life presents opportunities to argue or prove yourself right? What happens in your mind, body, and spirit when this occurs?

GODWARD REFLECTION

If we consider Jesus to be God, then it seems to follow that he would always be right. In this case, it doesn't seem like Jesus went out of his way to correct those who were wrong or to make a scene. What might this say about God?

PRAYER OF INTENTION

Write a prayer of intention about who you want to be in the face of an argument and the pressure to prove yourself right.

DAY 11: DO I JUSTIFY MYSELF WITH OTHERS' PAIN?

Luke 13:1-5

REFLECTION

SOMEONE TOLD Jesus the shocking news. Roman soldiers had killed a group of worshippers on the temple grounds. Then, someone in the circle wondered if this might have been a Divine consequence for their sin. Jesus responded, "Do you think they suffered because they were worse than you?" Then he mentioned another disaster that killed eighteen and repeated himself. "Do you think they were worse offenders than all the others living in Jerusalem?" With a stern rebuke, Jesus shut the conversation down. "Unless you repent, you will all perish just as they did."

"Unless you repent..." Those of us shaped by the assumptions of Evangelicalism tend to hear this passage as a formula for getting on God's good side or even gaining entry to heaven. Revival language comes to mind: Repent of your sins. Ask Jesus into your heart. Get saved so you won't perish eternally. Repent. Don't Perish. But in this scene, Jesus isn't having a conversation about salvation.

Generally, Rome gave the Jewish people wide latitude in their religious practice, so what might have caused these soldiers to violate the temple grounds and human lives in this way? Had the Romans uncovered a cell of insurgents? Had there been an act of violent rebellion that stirred up the Romans? Anti-Roman sentiment had been growing in Judea. Militant resistance would escalate for decades until Titus and the 10th Legion delivered Rome's retribution in 70 CE, leveling the temple, burning the city, and slaughtering thousands of residents and Passover pilgrims. With this historical context in mind, some commentators wonder if Jesus was warning the citizens of Jerusalem away from a path of violence that could only end in catastrophe.*

Regardless of what took place, Jesus' response to this question points to a common reaction that surfaces in the face of tragedy. It seems to be the case that many folks want to believe God controls every detail of existence because the discomfort of an uncertain world is intolerable. We don't want to imagine bad things happening to those we love, so we buy into the idea that God protects good people from harm.

---

* Brian Zahnd takes this tack. Writing on this passage, he said, "What is Jesus saying? Is he talking about Galileans and Judeans going to hell? Yes and no. Jesus isn't talking about a postmortem spiritual hell, but an impending literal hell. Jesus has been calling Jerusalem into the kingdom of God and the way of peace by the practice of enemy love and radical forgiveness. But for the most part Jerusalem has rejected this message of peace, believing instead that when the time comes God will fight with them in a war of independence and help them attain freedom by killing their enemies. In response to this enormously dangerous holy war assumption, Jesus warns Jerusalem against resorting to violence by telling them that if they don't rethink war and peace according to the kingdom of God, they're all going to die by Roman swords and collapsing buildings." Zahnd, Brian. *The Unvarnished Jesus: A Lenten Journey* (p. 82). Kindle Edition.

When terrible things happen, this theology requires validation. So, we blame the victim.

The only explanation that preserves our certainty is that terrible things happened to those people because of what they did. This perspective lies behind comments like, "They shouldn't have been doing that," or "She shouldn't have been wearing that," or "He should have just complied." The underlying assumption in these moments is that the terrible thing we've witnessed won't happen to those who've done right, played by the rules, or been suitably devout. "I wouldn't dress that way, so that would never happen to me. I'm just not that kind of person." If we can find a reason why the bad thing happened, we feel safe, and even justified in our views.

Rubbish, the lot of it. Jesus shuts the conversation down by pointing the questioners back to their own lives. It's as if he was saying, "Stop saying these people deserved what happened to them. Repent from this kind of blame-seeking! Focus on your own heart instead. There's plenty there to occupy your attention."

There is no shortage of contemporary applications of Jesus' words. When bad things happen, we want to know why. If we can attach the guilt to the victim, we wrap the tragedy up in a nice bow. Yes, something terrible happened (thoughts and prayers!), but it happened because of what they did. This leaves us feeling that the universe might just be manageable.

Jesus doesn't leave his followers such a convenient escape hatch. Love your neighbor as yourself. The Apostle Paul reframed Jesus' words by saying that we obey "the law of Christ" when we bear one another's burdens.* Loving a victim never looks like blame. Bearing the burden of someone

---

* "Bear one another's burdens, and in this way you will fulfill the law of Christ." Galatians 6:2, NRSVue.

injured in a tragedy never looks like distancing or theologizing about pain. When we blame the victim, we reveal that we are stuck in a fearful world of self-righteousness, where we secure our own sense of safety at the expense of others. Self-justification like this always results in the destruction of others, of community, and ultimately of ourselves. It is the path toward perishing. Exactly the sort of thing Jesus would invite us to repent from.

INWARD REFLECTION

Reflect on a time when you experienced a tragedy. What would it have looked like if those around you had "loved their neighbor as themselves?" Maybe someone did. What was that like? If no one did, what would have helped you feel seen and cared for?

GODWARD REFLECTION

Reflect on Jesus' response to the question of whether or not the victims of this tragedy had sinned. He tells the questioners to consider their own lives. In this moment, how might God be speaking to you from this text?

PRAYER OF INTENTION

Consider if there are any people (individuals or people groups) that you believe deserve the tragedy that has happened to them. Write a prayer inviting the Spirit to guide your heart as you relate to people like this so that your own natural feelings can come into alignment with the way of Jesus.

DAY 12: AM I DRAWN TO DESTRUCTIVE LEADERS?

John 10:1-21

REFLECTION

You've certainly seen one of those kitschy paintings featuring Jesus as a shepherd. Occasionally, it's a close-up, the lamb, fuzzy and vulnerable. Jesus' expression compassionate. Other times, the artist frames a wide shot. Jesus is walking amidst his flock. In one arm, he's cradling a lamb. In the other, he carries a crooked shepherd's staff. There's no evidence Jesus was involved in animal husbandry, yet this is a favorite theme in Christian art. It's an old theme, too. Three surviving examples of Christian catacomb art portray Jesus as a shepherd. One of these may be the oldest art depicting Jesus!*

The imagery came not from Jesus' historical career but

---

* You can see these three ancient images here: https://aleteia.org/2019/05/12/three-of-the-oldest-images-of-jesus-portrays-him-as-the-good-shepherd/

from a sermon recorded in John's Gospel. There, he calls himself "the Good Shepherd." Outside the gospels and sermons, that phrase persists as the name of hospitals and churches. As familiar as this image is, it's not a very helpful metaphor for many of us today. At least, not at first. Most of us are not farmers. Most have little experience with livestock. Without that experience, we're left to fill the phrase with meaning drawn from places like those Sunday school paintings of Jesus overlooking a pasture, snuggling a little lamb. The image is peaceful and calm, a nap-time Jesus.

If we look deeper, though, something here proves helpful in our modern world. In the Ancient Near East, the shepherd was a common metaphor for a king.* In Jewish scripture, it also was a label for the Messiah.† You may recall that David, the archetypal king of Israel, was a shepherd. Both the Psalms and the prophet Micah suggested that the Messiah would be in the mold of David. Like a shepherd, the Messiah would provide for and protect the people.

When Jesus preached that sermon, identifying himself as "the good shepherd," the audience knew all about the connection between shepherds and kings. If you had a good king, there'd be safety and peace, but mostly, kings took what they wanted for themselves. This audience also knew a bit about messiahs, as well. The increased suffering under Roman occupation and the long-standing hope for God's rescue through a chosen Messiah created an environment rich with

---

* For example, in *The Illiad*, written contemporaneously with some of the Hebrew Scriptures, Homer used the language of shepherd for kings multiple times. Akkadian literature identified kings as those selected to be "shepherd of the country." In his famous code, Hammurabi claims that the shepherding of his people was given to him by his god.

† Most famously, Psalms 23. Also consider Psalms 78, Isaiah 40 and Micah 5 as examples.

expectation. Before and after Jesus, several religious and political zealots gathered bands of warriors intent on overthrowing the Romans. These roving bands of armed men supported themselves in the same way disenfranchised armed men have always done — robbery and extortion. Supposedly, they were freedom fighters committed to the good of the nation. Practically? They were violent, and with Roman retribution, they brought violence in their wake.*

Listen again to Jesus' words about being the Good Shepherd through the lens of this metaphor of kingship. The Good Shepherd knows the sheep, and they know him. They are not anonymous peasants bowing and scraping to their ruler. The Good Shepherd is not a "hired hand" with no connection to the sheep, motivated only by personal gain. The Good Shepherd provides what is necessary for life and safety, good pasture, and abundant life. Others in the position are in it to steal, kill, and destroy. They bring death and run away at the first sign of danger. Unlike those mercenary kinds, the Good Shepherd lays down his own life for the sheep.

Israel understood life under puppet kings, demagogues, and political priests jostling for power. They lived under the suspicious eye of the Roman legions. They experienced the periodic and unpredictable violence of nationalist zealots who claimed their violence was necessary to restore their great nation. The people needed something different: a leader who led them in the way of peace.

Even if we don't use this word much anymore, we still seek shepherds. Whether in the next presidential election or in our desire to follow coaches, culture shapers, and

---

* The most famous of these was Simon bar Kokbha in the 5th century, who led rebels in the third Jewish-Roman war. Closer to the time of Jesus, there were men like Simon of Peraea (died, 4 BCE), Judas of Galilee (died, 6 CE), and Theudas (died, 46 CE).

influencers, we want to associate with strong leaders who can help us get where we wish to go. Even churches hire pastors who seem compelling under stage lights and can run the show behind the scenes.

Perhaps this is a human thing. We want leaders to help cut the edge of our uncertainty. There's a cost for this benefit. Following these people gives them power and prestige. We transfer some of our autonomy and personal responsibility to them. They make the hard choices for us. Then, if they fail, well, we were just "following the leader." Trusting a leader saves us an enormous amount of mental energy.

Because we so often desire this mental reprieve, and because there are many whose ego draws them into the role, we are inundated with calls to action from those who want to lead us. When we feel afraid or uncertain, choosing a shepherd seems pragmatic, another area where the ends justify the means. If a leader can get us where we want to go, does their character matter that much? But we can't escape accountability.

The voice of the Good Shepherd sounds different from this. No coercion. No manipulation. No use of fear to bring about a preferred outcome. Any trustworthy spiritual leader will have a voice that echoes the tone of the Good Shepherd.* This kind of leader will put the needs of their people first† and will intimately know them and their needs.‡ This kind of

---

* Another reason we are sometimes drawn to leaders who are destructive for us is our own unresolved trauma. If we grew up with abusive, or narcissistic, or even neglectful parents, then we have deeply rooted expectations of leaders that are unhealthy. If you find that you have a history of being drawn to leaders and even partners who are abusive, that may indicate the presence of unhealed trauma in your life. This is worth talking about with a trained trauma therapist.
† See John 10:11.
‡ See John 10:15.

leader won't let folks fall through the cracks or go missing.* The character of those leaders will shape the outcome of their leadership. We become more and more like the people we follow. That means choosing to follow a leader is a moral choice with significant implications for our character and the shape of our world.

INWARD REFLECTION

What kind of leader have you often been drawn to? How does this kind of leader compare with the voice and actions of the Good Shepherd?

GODWARD REFLECTION

If Jesus' "Good Shepherd" language describes how God leads and cares for us, how does this change your image of God?

PRAYER OF INTENTION

Write a prayer of intention about how you choose leaders and what kind of leader you want to be when you are in positions with influence.

---

* See Luke 15:4.

DAY 13: DO I DESPISE THE LITTLE ONES?

Matthew 18:10-14

REFLECTION

IF YOU'VE SPENT any time in church, you've heard the parable of the lost sheep. Heck, you may have even heard it referenced outside the church. Jesus talks about a shepherd who leaves the ninety-nine sheep safe at home to find that one lost, wandering sheep. Great story.

That story shows up in two different gospels, Luke and Matthew. Chances are you've only ever heard it presented in the context offered by Luke. See, in Luke's Gospel, the Lost Sheep is part of the trilogy of parables about lost things — a coin, a sheep, and a son. All three parables point to God's desire to find and recover those who are lost. If you grew up in or around Evangelical Christianity, that word carries a bunch of freight. In that world, "lost" means "not saved," as in "someone who hasn't received Jesus as their Lord and Savior and thus won't be going to heaven when they die." Sometimes folks in that community hear the word "lost" and think "damned." But that's not really what Matthew's Gospel is discussing.

In Matthew's telling of the story, Jesus tells this parable in a conversation about the "little ones."* Just before this story, Jesus' disciples had asked Jesus about greatness. Isn't that the question of our age? Is our country great? Is our military the greatest? Is my political candidate the greatest? Who is the greatest in my field? We want our kids to go to a great college. We want to eat great food. We want our lives to be great. Everything must be great!

Even if we don't think of ourselves as obsessed with these things, we still are drawn to "greatness" in other ways. We want our church to be influential in the community. We hope to be a part of important causes. We can't seem to tear our eyes away from bigness or greatness. In our culture, those qualities are seen as self-validating proof of success, maybe even evidence of God's blessing.

The parable of the lost sheep in Matthew's Gospel stands in opposition to all of this. The passage opens with Jesus admonishing, "Take care that you do not despise one of these little ones." Why would we despise a "little one?" Because they are not big! A little child isn't fully grown. What do they

---

* In his reflection on this same passage, Brian Zahnd drew my attention to the contrast between "greatness" and "littleness" in this sequence of stories. Three times in Matthew 18, Jesus talks about the "little ones." Because of the context, we often think this phrase refers to little children; after all, at the beginning of the chapter, Jesus was dealing with kids. But in Greek, there are several words that mean child, and the author of Matthew did not use any of them in these three instances. Where our English translation gives us the phrase "little ones," the Greek word is μικρός, or *mikros*, the origin of our modern prefix *micro-*. In 1st century Greek, this word could be used to describe children, but it had a much wider range and was more frequently used to mean other things, including little in size, little in degree, or low in status. Very often, it carried the connotation of unimportant.

know? What power or influence do they have? We transpose this same prejudice into other areas of life. A little church must not be blessed by God. A small-time writer must not have anything worthwhile to say. A little-known non-profit probably won't make much of a difference in the world. We despise the little ones precisely because they are not big.

Jesus uses the image of a shepherd going off in search of one lost little sheep to shift our vision. The large flock is safe, but the shepherd's attention is on the one little lamb who is lost and alone. It's easy to overlook, but in Matthew, this little parable is presented as the answer to the disciple's question, "Who is the greatest in the kingdom of heaven?"

The greatest, according to Jesus, is the one who will step away from the big flock to go and find the little wanderer. The greatest is the one who notices the small details, like a single missing sheep in a crowd of a hundred. The greatest is the one who isn't willing to let someone fall through the cracks—whether from poverty, mental health, racial inequity, religious exclusion, or prejudice. The greatest is the one who "doesn't despise the little ones."

We live in a culture mad with lust for success, and bigness is its chief indicator. I hope this isn't too jarring to hear, but success and bigness are not evidence of God's presence. Nothing in the way of Jesus tells us to seek these things— just the opposite. Remember, Jesus is the one who said the first will last and the last will be first.* Our pursuit of big things can be why we unthinkingly trample on others. It can be the drive that drains us of spiritual vitality. It can be the very poison that corrupts our souls.

The "little ones" matter to God. This includes when you feel small, unsuccessful, or unnoticed. God sees you. You

---
* Matthew 20:16.

matter. The Divine presence pursues you to welcome and include you. Being found, or what we often think of as salvation, is about much more than one's state in eternity. It's also about belonging now.

This also includes the "little ones" around you. Children. People in your community who can't take care of themselves or could but have had that opportunity taken away by others. Any who might have wandered off and found themselves lost and alone. These people all matter. God sees them and invites you to care for them as well.

INWARD REFLECTION

Who or what are "the little ones" that God is asking you to care about in your life and circle? Once you've named the easy ones, push farther out. Who are the others, little according to the world, that may be difficult for you to care for but who God might be inviting you to notice? Who are you tempted to despise and why?

GODWARD REFLECTION

If the parable of the lost sheep is about God's intention to find and gather those who are lost and alone, what does this tell you about God's relationship with you and others? How does this shape your understanding of God?

PRAYER OF INTENTION

Write a prayer of intention about your own response to the "little ones" in and around your life who God cares for and who you are tempted to despise.

DAY 14: DOES CONCERN FOR MERIT KEEP ME FROM LOVING WELL?

Luke 15:11-32

REFLECTION

DURING HIS FINAL walk to Jerusalem, Jesus told a story. It may be the most important religious text in human history. We most frequently refer to it as the Parable of the Prodigal Son. A more accurate title would be the Parable of Two Lost Sons. Both are lost, just in different ways. I won't summarize the story because I'd have to tell you the whole thing. You ought to go and read it.*

This story does many things, but I'd like you to consider just one — Jesus turns our ideas about merit upside down. Since we were toddlers and learned we could shout, "Mine," the concept of merit has been of grave concern to most of us.

---

* The NRSVue offers a solid translation of the story. The Message offers a vibrant paraphrase. Read the passage slowly, if you haven't already. Then come back here for my reflection.

We want to know that people deserve what they have and what's coming to them. Partly, this is self-protective. We don't want a world where people can unfairly take away what we've earned. Sometimes, we apply our sense of merit to others and call it justice. When others are in need, some of us wonder if they deserve help. When we talk about God's judgment or even God's love, we often work hard to make sure it's evident that, in the end, people get what's coming to them.

Both sons in this story were caught in the mental web of merit, believing that they deserved what they imagined was coming to them. The one who took his inheritance and ran away believed it. After embarrassing himself and shaming his family, he knew he deserved nothing from his father. Maybe he had even disqualified himself from being part of the family! The other son, who worked hard in the fields, believed it. When he saw his wayward brother welcomed with joy and celebration, he was bitter. He would not condone an unmerited celebration!

Unlike both sons, the father wasn't thinking about merit at all. For him, what mattered was a loving connection. In this case, that loving relationship manifested in reconciliation. Can we, children of post-enlightenment materialism and modern free-market capitalism, even comprehend that love does not take its cues from merit?

The runaway son was surprised by love. He came home convinced his choices disqualified him from receiving his father's generosity. The only path of repair he could imagine was working hard somehow to earn the place of a lowly household servant. He expected to be treated as he deserved. The hard-working son was also surprised by love. He was convinced his faithful effort entitled him to his father's generosity. He expected to be treated as he deserved.

Both were wrong. These men both believed what

mattered most to their father was merit. Their choices and emotional reactions were rooted in what they believed about merit. For both, their ideas about merit impeded intimacy with their father and each other. Merit wasn't on the father's mind at all. What was? Love. And love — no matter how complicated and unfair it seems — is not apportioned and awarded to those who deserve it. The father loved his children simply because they were his children. He wanted to be in a relationship with them, regardless of their choices.

The best title for this story would be The Parable of the Irresponsibly Generous Father. The sons didn't expect his response. Their community would have raised eyebrows incredulously, whispering about how the father was abandoning wisdom and decorum. But Jesus wasn't telling a sweet story about a moving parenting moment. Jesus was talking about how our expectations and attachments to merit corrupt every relationship — even our ideas about God. In our actions and theology, we can either be committed to ensuring people get what they deserve, or we can be dedicated to loving well.

INWARD REFLECTION

How do your ideas about merit shape the way you interact with others? Are there ways you've chosen merit over love?

GODWARD REFLECTION

If this story was the only text you had to tell you about God, what would your picture of God be like? Is that different from the picture you hold now? If so, how? If God loves you wildly, with no regard for merit, what does that stir in you?

PRAYER OF INTENTION

Write a prayer of intention around who you sense God is inviting you to be (and what actions you might take) regarding the way you love those around you, whether you feel they are worthy of it or not.

DAY 15: AM I AVOIDING WHAT I ALREADY KNOW?

Luke 16:19-31

REFLECTION

JESUS' story about the Rich Man and Lazarus is one of his weirdest. This is another where you just have to read the whole thing for yourself. Do that, and then come back here.

Nowhere else in Jesus' words do we find such details about life after death. For some, that's the primary point. This odd little story becomes a manual about the logistics and geography of heaven and hell. Point one: Dead people are conscious of their bliss or torment! Point two: Sinners have no comfort or respite on the other side! Point three: See how terrible it is! Folks who read this story this way seem to think that knowing the structure of punishment and reward after death will be ample motivation to change people's behavior.

If you think that's the purpose of this story, then I propose you haven't understood it at all. This story is a parable. There's even some evidence it isn't original to Jesus!* This story takes the structure of a particular genre of ancient morality tale. In this formula, a rich and powerful person and a beggar die. In the afterlife, the tables are turned. This type of story is meant to motivate good behavior. In Luke's telling, however, Jesus changes the familiar tale just a bit, and in doing so, he changes the whole point. (And that point has nothing to do with what happens after you die!)

When, all too late, the rich man realizes his fate, he tries to intervene so his still-living brothers can avoid the same terrible outcome. He acts like he's discovered news they could never imagine: His brothers need to be kind to the poor because, as it turns out — at least as far as the parable is concerned — if you aren't kind to the poor, you end up in hellish torment for eternity.†

In parables, just like in well-crafted jokes, the bit that matters most is the closing line. Everything before sets you up emotionally so that the punchline hits you for the most impact. When the Rich Man asks Father Abraham to send Lazarus to warn his brothers, Father Abraham refuses. Why? Because he thinks they already have all the guidance they need. Apparently, none of this should be news to them! When the Rich Man presses his case, we get the punchline: "If they don't listen to Moses and the prophets, they will not be convinced even if someone rises from the dead."

---

* Here's an excellent article that digs into the idea of Jesus using an already existing folktale for his own purposes here, including sources for the similar story in both Egyptian and Jewish texts that predate Jesus. https://isthatinthebible.wordpress.com/2016/03/01/is-the-parable-of-the-rich-man-and-lazarus-a-fable-about-the-afterlife/

† Notice the rich man's solution. He wants to send Lazarus to warn the brothers. Even in death, this man cannot imagine a solution where he's not telling other people where to go and what to do!

Scripture brims with passages containing instructions, commandments, and warnings about caring for the people around us. There are laws in Deuteronomy requiring a social safety net for the poor. There are screeds from the prophets decrying the selfishness and oppression by those in power. Over and over, scripture affirms those who take care of widows and orphans. Then, along comes Jesus saying that whatever you do for the hurting, the left behind, the marginalized, the least, you are doing for him. There is evidence that at least some congregations in the early church had administrative structures and leaders specifically to raise support for those in need.

In contrast, scripture has no affirmation for hoarding wealth. There are no "Take care of Number One" passages you can quote. Money comes up in the Bible occasionally, but it's almost always in the context of how troublesome it can be for your spiritual life or how often the pursuit of it leads to exploitation.

Focus on the punchline, not the graphic novel illustrations of hell. To his original audience and us, Jesus makes the point that many are just not interested in listening to the guidance of scripture regarding taking care of those around us. If we aren't convinced to do this by the words of scripture we already have, why would a spectacular personal revelation change our minds?

We already know we should be generous. We already know we should stand with the oppressed. We know it's the right thing to do. But we also have reasons why we can't. "I don't feel led . . . " "I know that's an important cause; I'm just not called to it." "This isn't the right season for me to do this." "Once I save up enough, then I'll help." Like the Rich Man, we do what we want to do with miles of reasons explaining why what we did was proper and reasonable.

This parable is not about what happens when we die but rather how we choose to live. Jesus suggests that we don't need a special holy messenger, or even the miracle of resurrection, to tell us to do justice and love mercy. We've already gotten that information. The question that remains is whether we will listen.

INWARD REFLECTION

Take stock. Are there specific things you already know you should be doing that you aren't? Don't get overwhelmed, and certainly don't have a legalistic panic. You and I are limited. We can't do everything. Just invite the Spirit to highlight if there are things that you specifically, in this season, might step into that you already know are the right things to do. What are these, and why do you feel the way you do?

GODWARD REFLECTION

It seems like Jesus is saying that God has already provided all the necessary information for people to make choices about how they relate to others. How does this shape your view of God and God's interaction with humanity?

PRAYER OF INTENTION

In the story, the Rich Man wanted to warn his brothers so they would have time to choose a different way of living. For today's Prayer of Intention, write a note to yourself in the same spirit, inviting God to help you speak truthfully to your soul.

DAY 16: DO I ESCALATE RETRIBUTION OR FORGIVENESS?

Matthew 18:21-35

REFLECTION

ISN'T FORGIVENESS GREAT? I mean, I love being forgiven. It's the call to forgive others that raises questions, right? In Matthew's Gospel, Peter asked Jesus about this. How often should we forgive people who just don't seem to get it? Knowing that Jesus was a big fan of forgiveness, Peter suggested that maybe seven times was a good number. I expect he thought this generous. Jesus responded, "Nope. Try seventy times seven." That seems too much.

Jesus took advantage of the stunned silence to tell a story about a man forgiven an overwhelming debt by his master. After receiving such unexpected grace, that man ran into someone who owed him a bit of money. He demanded payment. The debtor couldn't pay, so he had the man who owed him money thrown into prison. Some of his peers saw this and were disturbed (of course!) and told their master. The master hauled the first guy back in, reinstated the overwhelming debt, and threw him into prison until he could pay it. I'm not sure how you pay a debt while in prison.

Taken separately, these two episodes paint a confusing picture of forgiveness. First, Jesus seems to say, "Just keep on forgiving." That sounds very compassionate, but immediately, our minds go to all the reasons why that's a terrible idea. What about toxic people who take advantage? What about abuse? What about church leaders who violate trust and then use passages like this to force good Christian people to forgive them? Doesn't a commitment to unending forgiveness open us up to every kind of violation?

Second, the parable mentioned forgiveness, but when you follow the plot, it doesn't seem like it's about forgiveness at all. The first servant is forgiven a massive debt, but when he tries to collect a trivial debt, his original debt is reinstated. Doesn't that mean he wasn't forgiven in the first place? If someone holds forgiveness over your head, expecting particular behavior in response, that's a transaction, not forgiveness. That seems to mean the moral of the story is that if you don't forgive others, God will reinstate all your debts and punish you. Is that what Jesus meant?

There may be something deeper to consider. Turns out, this parable is not a manual on forgiveness. Peter offered forgiveness up to seven times. Jesus escalated that to seventy-times-seven. Those numbers aren't unique to this conversation. In the early part of Genesis, there's the story of Lamech, the son of Cain.* He brashly declared that if anyone

---

* I'm indebted here to Brian Zahnd, who first drew my attention to this connection in his commentary on this passage. His reading completely shifted how I view this passage in a way that seems to align much more clearly with Jesus' teaching elsewhere. Here's some additional information about the background of this reading. "In the Septuagint, the Greek in this

were to do him or his family harm, he would seek vengeance, not seven times, but seventy times seven times. The odd phrasing Lamech uses is the same that Jesus uses! Is it possible Jesus answered Peter's question about forgiveness by reminding him of the impact of escalating violence?

If Jesus is taking Lamech's oath of retribution and subverting it, the point of this interaction changes. Jesus is proposing that when we are violated, there are two paths we can take. Like Lamech, we can escalate retribution, or we can escalate forgiveness. Those two paths take us to different destinations. Lamech's vow of escalating retribution is critical background to the flood narrative. Escalating retribution leads to more retribution, which finally results in the near extinction of humanity. Think of that famous maxim: "An eye for an eye will leave everyone blind."*

The parable makes more sense if this is in Jesus' mind. The first servant receives enormous forgiveness. This creates

---

phrase in Genesis is identical to the Greek that Matthew records Jesus using. The Septuagint was the only Greek translation of Hebrew scripture at the time of Jesus and the early church. It was 'the Bible' they would have been familiar with. It is likely that Peter derives his number from Scripture's frequent use of 'seven times' for avenging evildoers, first with reference to the Lord's protecting the life of Cain by threatening sevenfold avenging of anyone who would slay him (Gen 4:15; Lev 26:21, 28; Deut 28:25; Ps 79:12; Prov 6:31; cf. Luke 17:4). If this is correct, then Jesus' reply may allude to Genesis 4:24, to Lamech's use of seventy-seven times (ἑβδομηκοντάκις ἑπτά, lxx). Lamech appeals to *lex talionis* to reason that if Cain, who murdered his brother out of malice, could be avenged sevenfold, then his own avengement ought to be seventy-sevenfold, an exaggerated number, because he killed in self-defense. Likewise, Jesus exaggerates Peter's number, to emphasize that remission is boundless." Ardel Caneday, "Lavishly Forgive Sins in Order to Be Forgiven: Jesus' Parable of the Unmerciful Servant," The Evangelical Review of Theology and Politics 5 (2017): 17–32.

* Often attributed to Gandhi, but there's no original source I can find to verify this. The phrase shows up in many places, not least of which is the play, *Fiddler on the Roof*.

a new possibility for him. Would he pass that forgiveness on, allowing the forgiveness he received to generate more forgiveness? Or would he stop the flow of forgiveness by choosing retribution? In the parable, he chose retribution, which ended up hurting him more.

As teaching tools, parables rely on surprise and discomfort to get you to think about yourself in ways you'd rather not. Stand in the place of the first servant. Having received enormous forgiveness, what would you choose to put out into the world? More forgiveness or more retribution? Whatever you choose will escalate and replicate in your web of relationships. That decision matters.

Necessary caution: I don't think Jesus expects good Christians to ignore abuse. I don't think he's saying that every time we're injured, we ought to rush to forgiveness without dealing with the consequences of what happened. I suspect that if we rush to forgiveness without honestly naming the injury and, where possible, holding the perpetrator accountable, we might be using forgiveness to spiritually bypass the hard work of healing.

Consider what Jesus may be telling us about reality. Our choices impact the world. Our communities are shaped by cause and effect. When we do violence to others, they want to do violence in return. When we demand retribution, others demand retribution in return. In the same way, when we forgive, forgiveness releases more freedom and forgiveness. Brian Zahnd puts it succinctly: "Jesus saves the world by turning exponential revenge into exponential forgiveness."* Which world do we want to live in?

---

* Zahnd, Brian. *The Unvarnished Jesus: A Lenten Journey* (pp. 43-44). Kindle Edition.

INWARD REFLECTION

Does anything about Jesus' story make you uncomfortable? Why do you think that is? How do you relate to the idea of forgiveness? (And be honest! There are lots of ways forgiveness is talked about that are unhealthy, even abusive. What has been your experience and why?)

GODWARD REFLECTION

In what ways can a model of escalating forgiveness be seen in the story of Jesus? What does this tell you about God?

PRAYER OF INTENTION

Write a prayer of intention around your posture toward forgiveness. How might you become the kind of person who escalates forgiveness?

DAY 17: DOES GOD-TALK KEEP ME FROM GOD?

Matthew 19:13-15

REFLECTION

God-talk can be such a trap. More and more time spent discussing, debating, and theologizing is often unhelpful — especially for good religious people who want to do the right thing. Here's what I mean.

As Jesus grew in fame, inevitably, some parents wanted to bring their children to Jesus for a blessing. In one episode in Matthew's Gospel, the disciples thought this was not a good use of Jesus' time and blocked the way. Jesus corrected them with the now famous line: "Let the little children come to me, and do not stop them; for it is to such as these that the kingdom of heaven belongs."*

This verse has inspired unending posters and paintings on the walls of church nurseries, but does it say anything more?

---

* Matthew 19:14, NRSVue.

In Matthew's Gospel, this little interaction stands out like an isolated island in the text. It's sandwiched between two much more important "grown-up" conversations. Is this important?

Just before this, Jesus was approached by a committee of religious people asking his opinion on divorce. Then, as now, this was a touchy topic. Even in Jesus' time, there were liberal and conservative groups that disagreed on whether divorce was acceptable. In response to this question, whatever Jesus said would undoubtedly offend someone. (Sound familiar?)

Whether in the ancient world or today, when religious people debate divorce, rarely does anyone notice that this isn't an abstract concern. Every divorce involves real people. Most who divorce are in deep pain, dealing with disappointment and loss. Some are trying to escape abuse. Then, even more than now, divorce would leave women without much social and economic protection. This debate had implications for real people's lives, bridging the gap between social justice and theology. Then, just after the scene with the children, there's another significant theological discussion. An influential young man approached Jesus, asking, "What must I do to have eternal life?" What could be more important than this? The young man thought he was a good person and said so. Jesus challenged him to go to a deeper and more self-sacrificial place. This was a conversation about personal morality and salvation.

These two conversations seem to encompass the whole of religion. On one side, we debate morality and standards, often ignoring the implications for hurting people. On the other side, we come to God asking self-centered questions about our righteousness and salvation. We want to be sure of God's will. (Maybe to make sure we're right?)

Matthew's Gospel places this scene with the kids between these two religious conversations. Is it any wonder the disciples wanted to keep the children away? Jesus had much more important things to do! But notice as Jesus explains the priority of God's attention. He says, "For it is to such as these that the kingdom of heaven belongs." Who is he talking about? The theologians intent on getting to the bottom of a controversy? The moral man seeking to justify himself? No. It's the children who simply want to be near Jesus.

This is challenging for me. I'm most comfortable in my head. I love to study, write, and articulate big ideas so people can grasp them. Not only that, but I also consider myself a generally good and compassionate person who is willing, in many cases, to sacrifice for others. I can easily feel like those things qualify me for Jesus' special attention. Reflecting on this sequence of stories, I am challenged to consider the things I think establish my belonging.

Jesus said, "Let the little children come." He said this is who the kingdom belongs to. What determines their belonging? A desire to be in Jesus' presence. The little children had nothing to offer but themselves. Jesus didn't say, "Bring me all your theological debaters, for the kingdom of God belongs to such as these." He didn't say, "Bring me all your self-righteous questions about salvation."

The theologians and moral police only came to Jesus to see if he was on their side, and the young man only came to Jesus seeking validation. All their God-talk wasn't about connecting with God at all. Perhaps it would be wise for us to take that as a warning.

INWARD REFLECTION

Do you notice times and places where God-talk and good religious intentions get in the way of your spiritual health? Why do you think that happens?

GODWARD REFLECTION

Consider Jesus' interactions in this scene. What do you see here that tells you about the nature of God's relationship with you?

PRAYER OF INTENTION

Write a prayer of intention about how you might be able to practice being more childlike in your pursuit of God.

DAY 18: DO I MEASURE OTHERS' RIGHTEOUSNESS?

Luke 18:9-14

REFLECTION

JESUS TELLS THIS STORY: Two men went down to the temple to pray. One of them was a notably religious person, devout, with a deep love for our way of life. The other was someone all agreed was a sinner, a blasphemer, and a collaborator with the enemy.

The religious person's prayer was mainly about himself. "I am so grateful," he prayed. For what was he grateful? The privilege and position God had given him? The presence of God in his life? The opportunities he had to serve? None of that. He was grateful that God hadn't destined him to be like certain other people: "Thieves, Rogues, Adulterers, or even this tax collector." Unlike those cast-outs, the religious person was a regular donor, which he noted in his prayer. He even went above and beyond in his spiritual practices! (Also noted.)

The other man was a tax collector. Although he had gone

to the temple to pray, he stood "at a distance." He knew the religious crowd didn't want him around. His prayer was short and straightforward. "God, be merciful to me, a sinner."

Jesus ends this odd little story by telling his listeners that (perhaps to the surprise of some) it was the tax collector who ended his prayer in good standing with God. God did not need to bother justifying the religious person. After all, they had spent the whole prayer justifying themselves.

How often do we look at others in ways that justify and elevate our rightness? This is the evil seed at the heart of every kind of purity culture. While the phrase "purity culture" is typically associated with conservative religious groups, the truth is that every group with beliefs and practices can fall into a purity culture mentality.* Ideological communities † form because they believe they know what leads to a better life. Their ideas may be good, rooted in a desire to alleviate harm or protect. Someone in their group notices that certain ideas, actions, and even words risk causing harm. That's when the evil seed blooms.

What may have begun as a thoughtful desire to protect from harm ends up mutating into a list of acceptable behaviors, words, and even thoughts. Knowing and adhering to this list becomes a tangible way to demonstrate we are on the side of What's Right. When we see others violate our list,

---

* Most often, this label is used to refer to the attitudes and practices of conservative Evangelical Christianity in regard to their teachings and practices around sexuality, but the dynamics cross into any group that thinks it has a "better way" and who shame those who violate the standard. Those who hew closely to the accepted standards are "pure" and everyone else is 'impure" and threatens the purity of the whole group.

† Any group that is held together by a shared system of beliefs runs this risk. This dynamic is not limited to religious groups but can be found in political parties, community groups, advocacy communities, and even health and wellness movements.

we must know why so we can begin categorizing the wrongdoers. Some transgress out of ignorance (the unconverted, the uninformed, the sheeple). Others violate our standards intentionally (the trolls, the deplorable, the Wicked.) Noticing those violations (Aha, I know the list!) and calling them out (See how courageous and committed I am!) validate our righteousness. We are certainly members of The Group, and why wouldn't we be? We're Right and only want to do What's Best For Everyone! What began as a reasonable and constructive belief becomes an identity marker we must defend at all costs. Truly, the human heart can turn any good thing into self-justification.

It's interesting to note, in Jesus' story, the awareness present in each person's prayer. The religious person addressed God, but their prayer seemed mainly aware of others. The prayer itself is a form of comparing and competing. By contrast, the prayer of the man everyone agreed was a sinner seemed only aware of himself and God. Even then, his self-awareness was of his own weakness.

I find myself vacillating between these two characters. Some days, my inner life bursts with the toxic gasses of comparison and competition. I should be further along in life than I am. Why didn't my book sell as much as that person's book? I can't believe those Christians think those absurd and offensive thoughts. (See how much more spiritual and evolved I am!) Other days, I can't see those things at all, and I don't want to. I am overwhelmed with my weakness, grief, and inability to change the world. All I can do is breathe out the Holy Name, trusting, or hoping, that God is at work.

In this short story, Jesus warns us away from comparison and competition, the inevitable trap of self-justification that lies at the door for any one of us who believes deeply in a better way of life. He tells us that God is near to the brokenhearted, present with those who know themselves as weak. Using our best beliefs and commitments to devalue and dehumanize others to feel secure is a failure to love and a betrayal of those good beliefs.

INWARD REFLECTION

The religious person's prayer started with, "Thank God I'm not like . . ." and then listed off folks who made him shudder. Take an honest inward glance. Are there people or groups that you sometimes feel this way about? Why do you think that is?

GODWARD REFLECTION

Scan the story again and note your sense of what it says about God and God's perspective toward us. While the story has an ethical angle for how people relate to one another, consider how Jesus' words might show us more of the nature of God.

PRAYER OF INTENTION

Write a prayer of intention reflecting on how you might tangibly identify and redirect yourself away from the temptation of performance and comparison in your spiritual life and toward focusing on your own pursuit of God.

DAY 19: ARE MY THINGS IN MY WAY?

Mark 10:17-31

REFLECTION

A YOUNG MAN approached Jesus for advice. He was privileged, wealthy, and influential. He wanted to know what he needed to do to fully participate in the new kind of life Jesus was preaching. By his own report, he'd been a good person. He observed all the religious practices. So, why did he end up leaving his conversation with Jesus disappointed?*

Mark's Gospel says he went away shocked and grieved because "he had many possessions." What he had (or perhaps his attachment to what he had) made Jesus' words seem impossible. This is a tense passage for many of us. It suggests that something quite natural can impede our ability to follow

---

* This story is presented in three of the Gospels (Matthew, Mark and Luke). Not every story of Jesus is preserved in multiple gospels. When one is, it tells us that the early church saw this story as crucial to pass on.

Jesus. As humans, we are self-interested. We are drawn to that which will make us secure. This is nowhere more obvious than when it comes to our relationship with what we own.

Reflecting on this passage, Brian Zahnd notes, "The truth is that for most of us, economic self-interest is the single greatest obstacle to full participation in the kingdom of God."* This view is unpopular today. Many modern Christians don't know this was a point of broad agreement in the church for a long time.

Consider these words from three influential early preachers: Ambrose wrote: "You are not making a gift of your possessions to a poor person. You are handing over to him what is his."†

St. Basil‡ preached:

> It is the hungry man's bread that you withhold, the naked man's cloak that you have stored away, the shoe of the barefoot that you have left to rot, the money of the needy that you have buried underground . . .§

Two hundred years later, Gregory the Great wrote:

---

* Zahnd, Brian. *The Unvarnished Jesus: A Lenten Journey* (p. 16). Kindle Edition.
† Ambrose, one of the most influential theologians in the early era of Christianity, became Bishop of Milan in 379 CE. This quote comes from a sermon called *De Nabuthe* ("On Naboth") (c. 12, n. 53).
‡ Basil of Caesarea was a Greek theologian who lived in the 4th century. He's one of the three theologians referred to as the Cappadocians who profoundly shaped how the church talked about the nature of Christ and the Trinity.
§ Thomas Aquinas (13th c., Italian Catholic philosopher and Scholastic theologian, probably the most important Christian writer in the Middle ages.) quotes this passage in the *Summa Theologiae*, Question 32 on Almsgiving, quoting a sermon by Basil on the Gospel of Luke.

> When we administer necessities to the needy, we give them what is their own, not what is ours; we pay a debt of justice, rather than do a work of mercy.*

Reflect on those words for long, and it just might turn your whole world upside down. I was born and bred in a culture that venerates capitalism from top to bottom. Most folks around me considered capitalism an unarguable good and a non-negotiable commitment. Whether we are defenders or critics of capitalism and its impact, we'll likely all agree that economic self-interest is the engine that drives it.

Whatever good this economic system has offered the world — and it certainly has done good — it does seem that the motivating principle of economic self-interest makes it very difficult for us to love our neighbor as ourselves. Maybe we just don't want to share our resources. We worked hard for what we have! We deserve all of it, right? Or, maybe we have some extra and are willing to share, but the same motivation leads us to need to qualify the folks who receive our generosity. We create categories like "the deserving poor."

It's hard to make a case from the teaching of Jesus that accumulated wealth is anything other than a spiritual obstruction. My immediate gut reaction is honestly a lot of self-justification. "Well, I'm not rich. I mean, we're barely middle class . . ." That's an interesting game of relativity, isn't it? Can my family freely spend money whenever we want on anything we want? No, but an objective accounting of our standard of living puts my family into the top percentages of wealth worldwide. I don't feel rich, but if I asked a single

---

* Gregory was a theologian who became Pope in 590 CE. He was profoundly influential on pastoral theology. His book, *The Pastoral Rule*, was the essential guide for priests for a thousand years. This quote is found in Book III, Chapter 21.

parent working three jobs with no days off, or people sleeping in one of Portland's homeless encampments, or war refugees their opinion on my family's financial status, I'd probably get a different perspective.

For folks like me who've had mostly a life of economic stability, it may be important to remember: Jesus' injunction wasn't "accumulate until you're middle-class and then love your neighbor as yourself." Paul didn't write, "Fully fund your retirement, your kid's college fund, and your vacation savings account and then bear one another's burdens and so fulfill the law of Christ." Why not?

Money and material things have a way of owning us. They certainly shape our options. They can limit the possibilities we imagine. Oddly, the more we accumulate, the more self-protective many of us become. Without meaning to, we can find ourselves driven by our relationship to these things. That can manifest as a persistent need to save, plan, and horde. Just as easily, it can show up as a need to spend our money while we have it. In either case, our sense of identity is poisoned, and our ability to be generous is compromised.

Like that young man, we wonder how we can best find the life Jesus offers. One part of Jesus' invitation, perhaps painful, is letting go of identity-forming attachments to material things. Only then can we truly follow Jesus with all of our lives.

INWARD REFLECTION

Are there ways in which your attachment to certain material things impedes your ability to love others well?

GODWARD REFLECTION

Why might God be interested in your relationship to money and material things?

PRAYER OF INTENTION

Write a prayer of intention around the place of money and material things in your spiritual life.

DAY 20: IS MY IMAGE GETTING IN MY WAY?

Mark 10:46-52

REFLECTION

JESUS and his convoy passed through the ancient town of Jericho on their way toward Jerusalem. In Jericho, a crowd gathered to see this famous teacher and healer. In the crowd was a man who was blind. His name was Bartimaeus.

When Bartimaeus heard Jesus passing by, he made a scene. He cried out. He begged for healing. Some in the crowd thought his behavior wasn't fitting. Not a good representation of their town for a visiting hero! They tried shutting Bartimaeus up, but he cried out even louder. His scene worked! Jesus asked for him to be brought over and asked, "What do you want me to do for you?" Bartimaeus asked for his sight, and Jesus healed him, saying, "Go; your faith has made you well."

Notice the concern of the crowd. Having an influential person like Jesus visit was a big deal. The impression they wanted to give didn't include shouting beggars. (Think of the lengths modern cities go to hide their homeless population when the Olympics come to town.) Notice also that the crowd wasn't concerned about Bartimaeus' needs. They'd all seen him begging on the corner. They knew what he needed. Yet, it doesn't seem to have occurred to them that this was an opportunity for his healing. They didn't help him to the front of the crowd or try to draw Jesus' attention. They just wanted him to stop making noise.

Contrast that with Bartimaeus. An opportunity arose for him to get what he needed, but he had to make a scene to get it. He had to push past the social pressure of those around him who wanted him to take up less space. He had to ignore the whispers of people looking down on him with pity disguised as compassion. He had to interrupt the proceedings. That took enormous courage.

This contrast seems important. In the crowd, I see a mirror. Can I see them in myself? Am I attached to appearing as if everything is fine? Do I need to be in control, making every situation seem smooth and proper, without unsightly chaos? Is image management keeping me from noticing the needs of people around me?

The Jericho crowd didn't want to look like rubes, who didn't know how to host an influential visitor. The concerns of the crowd meant they didn't find what they were after. Only one person did. Bartimaeus didn't have the luxury of worrying about what others thought of him. He was desperate for an encounter with Jesus — and it wasn't even for the spiritual reasons we often applaud! He wasn't asking for spiritual maturity or salvation. He had a profound need and was desperate for help. He had to step out beyond his fear of what others thought of him.

Image attachment, control issues, and cynicism are all

self-protective postures we adopt because we don't want to look dumb or naive or be taken advantage of. After all, we won't look stupid if we don't put ourselves out there. Perhaps, though, there is a cost to these measures. In this story, who are the truly blind ones?

INWARD REFLECTION

I mentioned seeing the crowd as a mirror. When you look at their attitude and behavior, do you see anything instructive about yourself? Are there ways that similar concerns are limiting your experience of God or your ability to participate in God's liberating work in the world?

GODWARD REFLECTION

Consider Jesus' response to the crowd and Bartimaeus. What does this tell you about the nature of God?

PRAYER OF INTENTION

Write a prayer of intention on the image issue and how you relate to how other people see you. If you sense a holy invitation, include a tangible step you can take to make a change.

DAY 21: DO I INVALIDATE OTHER PEOPLE'S IDENTITY OR SPIRITUAL EXPERIENCE?

John 9:1-41

REFLECTION

JESUS and the disciples come across another blind man. This one had been born without sight. This is another healing story, but it's also a catalog of ways we can be terrible to people in the name of God.

When the disciples noticed this man, they started debating the cause of his tragedy. "Who sinned?" They asked. "This man or his parents?" I love discussing theology. Maybe you do, too. Have you noticed that sometimes, our theological discussions turn people into topics? "Terrible, this man's situation. But why did it happen? Was God punishing him? Or possibly his parents? Let's discuss the nature of evil, shall we?" Frankly, it's dehumanizing.

After Jesus healed this man, the man's neighbors couldn't believe it was really him. They didn't recognize him since he wasn't begging. The man's disability was all they could see.

He had to argue with them about his identity! The religious leaders were so sure that God wouldn't intervene in this guy's life that they dragged in his parents to determine once and for all if he was who he said he was. They didn't trust the man to tell his own story. His experience didn't fit their preconceptions, so they would not accept his identity. There's a long, long line of women, disabled people, queer people, people of color, and many other folks, all nodding heads in recognition, having been put in this same position by Christians who want to debate the truth of their experience.

None of this aligned with the religious power holders' expectations and understanding of God. They were so deeply opposed to Jesus that they could not conceive of the possibility that Jesus had healed the man. Healing blindness was rare, so it was considered something only God could do. If they admitted Jesus had healed this man, they would have to accept that Jesus was more than an ordinary teacher.

So, they assumed the healed man must be lying. Then, when they had no option but to admit he had been healed, they tried to debunk the miracle, looking for some other means by which Jesus had done it. They were committed to a preconception of how God would work. Because of this, they had to discredit the man's encounter with Jesus. Finally, when the man who was healed would not recant his story, the religious leaders decided he was guilty by association. So they kicked him out of their group. He would not accept their authority by submitting to their narrative about his life, so they excommunicated him.

There's one last ironic exchange. After the episode wraps up, Jesus comments about how his work would bring sight to some who are blind, but others who think they can see will be blinded. Some religious leaders overheard this quip and, with a profound lack of self-awareness, said, "What? Is he saying we can't see? That makes no sense at all."

This chapter in John's Gospel reads like a "greatest hits" of how religious people invalidate the spiritual experience of people who live outside their box. Consider it a fair warning. How do we relate to those whose experience of life and God doesn't fit our template? Have you seen or experienced any of these? We dehumanize people by turning their tragedy into a debate. We blame victims. We disregard the personal experiences of those who don't fit our views. We invalidate people's sense of identity if we don't like where they end up. We simply don't believe the spiritual experiences of people outside our particular spiritual stream — even other Christians. We demand people prove their experiences to us.

When these people won't accept our judgment or submit to our narrative, we shun them, kick them out of fellowship, or otherwise declare they are the worst kind of sinner. When someone dares to challenge us on this behavior, we can't even imagine we were wrong. We're good people. We're right about God! How could we be the ones who can't see?

It doesn't have to be like this. If we think the way of Jesus is life, why would we do harm as a result of our beliefs? If we believe in God's grace and mercy (even while "we were yet sinners"), how could we relate to others in any other way? If the guiding ethic that Jesus gave us is "Love your neighbor as yourself," how could we treat our neighbors in ways we would never accept being treated ourselves?

INWARD REFLECTION

There's a good chance you've been on one side or the other of this equation. Have you been on the receiving end of this kind of invalidation? What was that like? Or (if you're willing to be honest) have you been responsible for invalidating the spiritual experience of others? How did this experience impact you and the others involved?

GODWARD REFLECTION

Contrast Jesus' interaction with the blind man with everyone else in the story. What do you see here? What does this tell you about God?

PRAYER OF INTENTION

Write a prayer of intention about how you want to relate to the spiritual experience and story of those around you, even people you disagree with. Perhaps consider how you've felt when others treated you as if your experience was invalid.

DAY 22: AM I OFFENDED BY GENEROSITY?

Matthew 20:1-16

REFLECTION

THIS PARABLE IS VEXING. A quick summary: The farm owner decides to pay his workers in a way that feels unfair. The workers who worked an hour get paid the same as those who worked all day, and then the farm owner declares that he is in the right when some of the workers complain. Jesus makes no one happy here. Brian Zahnd commented, "If the parable came from anyone else, most American Christians would dismiss it as Marxist propaganda."* There are stacks and stacks of interpretations that wildly disagree with each other, revealing the distance we've gone to manage the offense of the parable. Read the parable for yourself, and, as much as possible, set aside preconceptions, noticing your reaction.

---

* Zahnd, Brian. *The Unvarnished Jesus: A Lenten Journey* (p. 49). Kindle Edition.

Some interpreters, looking from the perspective of those last-hour laborers, see this as a parable teaching grace. This interpretation often strips the economic aspect out of the parable, spiritualizing it. If the parable is about grace, the landowner is the hero — the God-figure — and those of us who have accepted God's grace are the last-hour laborers receiving something we didn't work for.*

Other interpreters, looking from the perspective of those early-morning-laborers, see this as a story about exploitation. In that reading, there is no hero or worthy God figure. The owner and the worker all fail to be their brother's keeper. The owner should have paid everyone a fair wage. The workers should have banded together to make sure everyone's needs were met. The proposal made following this reading is that in the Kingdom of God, economic exploitation doesn't happen, and we bear one another's burdens.

Still other interpreters merge these concerns for justice and grace together. For this reading to work, you've got to assume the amount paid to the early workers was not an exploitative wage. At the day's end, everyone was paid the same. Yes, that was unfair, but because of a high initial wage, this is a case of unfair benevolence. In this reading, the parable's judgment falls on the early morning workers, who are angry about this generosity. They seem to echo the actions and attitudes of the older brother in Luke's Lost Son parable. They have worked all day long. They have carried the load. Even though their pay is generous, they feel they've been mistreated.

Regardless of how you think this parable ought to be read,

---

* Some of these commenters think the late-comers are the "gentile Christians," anyone who came to follow Jesus after the initial circle who were all of Jewish background. Because of the tension between these two groups that we can see in Acts and Paul's letters, this reading is a reasonable one.

keep this in mind. Parables are designed to jar you, creating an unexpected chance to see yourself more accurately. Parables are mirrors; the truth they reveal is often found in our gut reaction to the story.

Take a moment to notice any discomfort in yourself. Do you jump into this parable in the place of the aggrieved workers? You're a hard-working early bird who's done more than your fair share, and those in power are taking advantage of you? Or do you see yourself as one of the late workers, just happy to have a job and thrilled by unexpected generosity? Maybe you identify with the landlord and think of yourself as choosing generosity, wondering why others don't think you're being fair. Where do you find yourself? Perhaps the parable can do its work in us if we can set the interpretive debates aside.

When I look into this mirror, I most often find myself as one of the bitter workers, thinking others are being given what I deserve. There are so many spreadsheets in my head calculating who is worthy and who is not — including myself. I've moved past this mindset in (most of) my theology, but I can still viscerally feel those scales tipping. Some days, I have to make a conscious decision to be generous. Sometimes, I have to decide to act in opposition to my discomfort at the idea of people getting something "for free" rather than worrying about whether they are taking advantage. This calculus of merit has been ticking away subconsciously my whole life. It feels like justice, but it's a self-justifying poison.

It's taking the slow work of grace and emotional healing for me to notice and (begin to) let this go. But that's what I see when I look into the mirror of this parable. Your experience may be different.

INWARD REFLECTION

Who do you see when you look into the mirror of this parable? How do you feel about that?

GODWARD REFLECTION

The different readings of this parable also open up differing views of God. Remember that this is a story told by Jesus, so whatever this parable says must be interpreted in light of what he taught about God. With that in mind, what does this story tell you about how God relates to us?

PRAYER OF INTENTION

After considering your gut reaction to this story (Connection? Confusion? Discomfort? Joy? Something else?), write a prayer of intention around what you believe God is addressing in your heart.

DAY 23: DO I TREAT SOME PEOPLE AS IRREDEEMABLE?

Luke 19:1-10

REFLECTION

AN UNFORTUNATE TENDENCY of religious communities across history is how easily they label certain people as irredeemable. One of the fastest ways for a religious leader to lose support is when they violate these community standards by accepting or including those who had previously been seen as outsiders. By the middle of Luke's Gospel, Jesus began to experience this. Yes, he was a charismatic teacher who could draw enormous crowds and somehow even provide food and heal the sick, but that couldn't make up for the way he violated some essential community standards and beliefs.

One of those? Table hospitality was a significant marker of blessing and respect in the Ancient Near East.* Some folks were uncomfortable, even indignant, that Jesus extended

---

* "Tax collectors and sinners were coming near to listen to him. And the

hospitality to those the community* had decided were unfit and unwelcome.

The story of Zacchaeus brings this to life. As a tax collector, Zacchaeus worked closely with the Romans. This made him ritually unclean. He served their imperial purposes, which made him a collaborator with the enemy. Like many tax collectors, it seems he had used his position to enrich himself at his neighbors' expense. This man, the community decided, was a great sinner. He wasn't getting invitations to dinner. He wasn't welcome in the worshipping community. He lived under the full weight of religious shunning.

Then Jesus came to town. Not only did Jesus notice and take Zacchaeus seriously, but he also requested an invitation to Zacchaeus' home. His words: "I must stay at your house tonight." I must! Surely, there were inns or homes Jesus could stay in that weren't so controversial? If Jesus was so intent on making a difference in Zacchaeus' life, wouldn't it have been better if he started with a confrontation? You know, a come-to-Jesus moment? "I'd very much like to stay with you tonight, but before we do that, you must repent!" But Jesus didn't seem concerned about his reputation or the success of his ministry.†

Pharisees and the scribes were grumbling and saying, 'This fellow welcomes sinners and eats with them.'" Luke 15:1-2, NRSVue.

* Or perhaps it was the leaders who had made this decision. There is enormous pressure in any community to fit in and be considered acceptable. If popular and trusted leaders decide that someone is "out" it's not uncommon for the community to follow.

† One of my beta readers, Heather, made this thoughtful observation about this "come-to-Jesus" moment. She wrote: "I wonder how much action-reaction was going on between Zacchaeus and his community. 'That guy steals all our money, stay away from him!' 'Those people always spit in my path; I'm going to jack up their bill next time!' Jesus broke the cycle by extending grace. I like to think that that was Zacchaeus's 'come-to-Jesus' moment. Well, really, it was Jesus's come-to-Zacchaeus moment. I like to

Even so, during his interaction with Jesus, Zacchaeus did repent. Not only did he commit to stopping what he had been doing, but without prompting, he committed to making reparations! He understood that by taking that money, he had also taken away the opportunity to use that money to make more money. So he paid back what he stole with 400% interest!

The end of the story is fascinating from a modern perspective. Jesus declares, "Today, salvation has come to this household!" Had the Gospel of Luke been written by a modern American Evangelical Christian, that sentence could not have been written. There's no record that Zacchaeus underwent a process where he "accepted Jesus as his Lord and Savior." There's no scene where he "invited Jesus into his heart" after confessing his sins and asking for forgiveness. We don't know the content of Jesus' and Zacchaeus' conversation, but we do know that the author of Luke's Gospel felt there was only one thing necessary to show us: a changed life. Zacchaeus takes personal responsibility, makes amends, and even pays reparations. We don't know precisely what he believed about Jesus. We only get to see a tangibly changed life.

Where do we see ourselves in this story? Are we among the indignant crowd wondering why Jesus is bothering with this self-absorbed, hateful man who has robbed so many of their dignity and livelihood? Are we standing with the devout religious people, concerned that Jesus might be throwing away his reputation and ministry impact by being associated with someone everybody knows is so terrible? How do we feel

---

think that Jesus's reckless grace shattered the blinders of Zacchaeus's spiraling retribution. No Bible-beating is necessary, just a mirror of grace and light to pierce the darkness in his heart . . . Ever the Shepherd, Jesus came to seek and save every last lost lamb. Even the ones up in trees."

about the apparent sinners in our lives, the people we and our community have written off because we think they are likely irredeemable? And then, how do we feel when Jesus actually redeems those people?

There is another question here that is, perhaps, more important. Did this turnaround in Zacchaeus' life happen because of something unique about his interaction with Jesus? Or is it possible that Jesus merely offered Zacchaeus something his community refused to offer?

INWARD REFLECTION

Are there people in your life — real people with names and faces that you've had genuine relationships with — that you've written off as irredeemable? Why?

GODWARD REFLECTION

What do Jesus' actions in this story tell you about God? What do they tell you about a healthy or unhealthy spiritual community?

PRAYER OF INTENTION

Write a prayer of intention around your relationship with the folks you consider irredeemable, and what this might mean for your actions.

DAY 24: AM I DRAWN TO POWER?

Mark 10:32-45

REFLECTION

IN THIS SCENE, we see the difference that often exists between our expectations and God's when it comes to how we achieve our goals. Jesus tells the disciples (one more time) about what will happen to him when he arrives in Jerusalem. They miss entirely (one more time) what he's saying. For them, heading to Jerusalem means occupying the seat of power. They fully expect Jesus to inaugurate a new order of things.

Not wanting to get left out, James and John pull Jesus aside and ask if they can have important positions in Jesus' new government. In retrospect, their request is absurd. The glory of God will be revealed, not on a golden throne, but on a bloody cross. Jesus reveals the unexpected: a God who invites rather than compels, who enters into our disgrace rather than retreating behind power. The cross is where God lets us throw our tantrum of violence, and rather than exploding with retribution, absorbs the pain and loss so that we can see a better way. Asking to sit at the left and right of Jesus' throne is to ask for martyrdom. They have no idea.*

James, John, and the other disciples were caught up in a common belief system: The only way to get good things done is by using coercive power.† With Jesus at the head of a new government, inspiring the troops and providing free food, they would push back the Roman occupiers and throw out the corrupt officials. In their sacred hands, good violence would push out bad. One way of reading human history suggests this is the only path forward, but this is not Jesus' path.

Looking at these misdirected disciples, I feel growing self-justification. I want to point at the world around me, naming names. Look at these Christian leaders who have fallen into the same trap, preaching that Christians' primary goal ought to be taking control of government to bring about God's will. Look at how we're compromising our witness with our single-issue stubbornness, hoping to solve one problem while

---

* It is worth noting that James ends up being an early Christian martyr. At some point, his understanding of the way of Jesus changed. Worth remembering that despite our normal human drives for comfort and self-protection, spiritual growth really is possible.

† Power, simply put, is the ability to make things happen. The question of ethics enters in when we consider the mechanism that allows things to happen, or people to be influenced. There are many academic schemes describing different types of power, but for my purposes here, we're considering that deeply human desire to want to "make" people do something and to push for that through a means that is something other than an open, honest invitation for consent. I use the phrase "coercive power" to refer to any attempt to influence that includes the pressure of manipulation, deceit, implied risk of punishment, or explicit threat of danger or violence, whether physical or emotional. Coercive power considers the autonomy and conscience of other people as an obstacle to be overcome.

ignoring a hundred others. Think of how often we've heard or said, "If only we could get more Christians into leadership in this company . . . in this city . . . in our school district . . . in this country!"

As my self-justification mounts, I'm conscious of something else. My intense desire to name those names obscures the temptation I feel myself. I also have a view of what a good society looks like. I also wish and pray for leaders who align with my views. And occasionally, when I see people doing things I disagree with, things I believe deeply hurt the community, I also want someone stronger to come along and slap them down.

Listening to James and John, I'm reminded that I, too, can get caught up in the belief that coercive power is simply a tool without moral valence, waiting for the right person to pick it up and use it. History and scripture both tell us this is an illusion. Coercive power, whether it manifests in manipulation or violence, has an energy, a kind of gravity, that inevitably changes the moral DNA of those who use it.* We're sure we're different. We are good and righteous, and surely that means we can pick up the Ring of Power without being corrupted.

The disciples certainly thought this, but Jesus challenged them. He told them that while it was normal for "the rulers of the world" to use the tools of domination, that was not how it should be for them. Then, he modeled this path. If Jesus is a revelation of the Father's nature, then we know something new about God that humanity didn't always know.† God is

---

* Maybe even biological DNA! We're still in the early stages of research, but the consequences of trauma seem able to be passed down to children. Epigenetics is the study of this process, and has demonstrated incredible possibilities for how we can carry traumatic history in our DNA.
† Brian Zahnd captures this in a bit I've heard him say in a handful of

not into coercion. God draws. God persuades. God invites. Those walking the other-centered, co-suffering way of Jesus are invited to this same commitment.*

INWARD REFLECTION

The temptation to use coercive power to get good things done is compelling. It's easier to see the lie when you've been coerced. Reflect on experiences you've had where other people manipulated or forced you to do what they wanted or when the threat of violence was used to get you to do something. How did it feel? How did it impact your relationship? How did it affect the way you thought about the outcome?

Note: If you are a survivor of relationship abuse or another situation where you experienced violence, take care of yourself as you reflect on this question. You don't need to relive your trauma to benefit from this reflection.

GODWARD REFLECTION

Our posture toward coercive violence is deeply connected to our picture of God. Some theological narratives depend on God's righteous violence. To build a mindset around the attitude of Jesus, though, we have to interrogate our pictures of God and the theology we hold. Take some time to think

---

sermons that also comes up in his book, *The Unvarnished Jesus*. He says, "God is like Jesus. God has always been like Jesus. There's never been a time when God was not like Jesus. We haven't always known this, but now we do." Zahnd, Brian. *The Unvarnished Jesus: A Lenten Journey* (p. 147). Kindle Edition.

* If the idea that there is a way to read scripture without attributing violence to God is new to you, and you'd like to learn more, I recommend two books by Dr. Bradley Jersak, *A More Christlike God* and *A More Christlike Word*.

about the theology you've been taught. Does it portray God as violent? How does it justify that violence? The Gospels show Jesus influencing individuals and a whole community without using coercive power, even when his life was threatened. What might this show us about the nature of God?*

PRAYER OF INTENTION

Write a prayer of intention concerning your temptations around coercion, manipulation, or even the threat of violence to accomplish good things.

---

* It is not sufficient to say that the God in Hebrew scripture, what Christians call the Old Testament, was one way (more violent), but Jesus came and made a change. The truth is that the mercy and long-suffering nature of God is present throughout Hebrew Scriptures as well. Jesus was revealing the heart of who God has been all along.

DAY 25: DO I EXPECT GOD TO BE ON MY SIDE?

Matthew 21:1-11

REFLECTION

AT THE BEGINNING of the week that would end with his death, Jesus entered Jerusalem like a hero. On the back of a donkey colt, at the head of a growing procession, he rode into Jerusalem. As he approached the city gates, people threw their cloaks onto the ground, an impromptu red carpet. Others waved palm branches like victory banners. Some shouted, "Blessed is the king who comes in the name of the Lord!" Others shouted, "Hosanna!"

The atmosphere was electric. It was Passover, one of the pilgrim festivals. Jerusalem was bursting with visitors from all around the Mediterranean. This was also the time of year when the people's nationalism ran hottest. Passover commemorated God's liberation of the Hebrew people from Egyptian slavery. The existing arrangement in Judea — a puppet king, excessive taxes for the privilege of being a

Roman province, and constant supervision by Roman legions — made the story of God's liberation from slavery feel especially relevant. Pilate, the provincial governor, was concerned that too many people were thinking about liberation. In response, he moved his personal legion into Jerusalem for the Passover season, just in case.

People crowding the streets, shouting praise and declaring a new king, all while Jerusalem is bursting with pilgrims, celebrating freedom from slavery? Any Roman official watching this unfold had to have been ready to push the panic button. Rome did not tolerate freedom movements. The religious leaders knew that if they did not solve the problem themselves, Rome would solve it for them — and Rome's solution might mean they lost their jobs!

Certainly, Jesus knew all of this. He asked his disciples to find the donkey colt. He knew this would bring to mind the prophecy of Zechariah. "Rejoice! Your king comes . . . riding a donkey . . ."* Jesus had been telling his followers all along that the Kingdom of Heaven had arrived. He was establishing a kingdom. But what were those people's expectations of his new kingdom? Think about the folks standing at the gate, lining the streets, cheering for Jesus. That makes them the good guys, right? They wanted Jesus to be king. They wanted their world to fall into line with Jesus' rulership. But what did they think that meant?

From the words of the disciples and Jewish writing from

---

* The whole passage is worth your attention. Imagine seeing Jesus enter Jerusalem in this way, knowing these words: "Rejoice greatly, O daughter Zion! Shout aloud, O daughter Jerusalem! See, your king comes to you; triumphant and victorious is he, humble and riding on a donkey, on a colt, the foal of a donkey. 10 He will cut off the chariot from Ephraim and the war horse from Jerusalem; and the battle bow shall be cut off, and he shall command peace to the nations; his dominion shall be from sea to sea and from the River to the ends of the earth." Zechariah 9:9-10, NRSVue.

the period, it seems clear that they imagined a powerful, independent nation. They remembered the legendary stories of the past: King David, King Solomon, back when Israel was great. They wanted foreigners out of power. They wanted to stop paying taxes to the empire. They wanted Rome out of their decisions. I imagine they wanted to feel pride in their nation again. They expected Jesus to turn the tables. He was coming to evict the corrupt. He was a king, but a king who was on their side. I suspect many of them weren't cheering for Jesus specifically; they were cheering for the idea that they would finally be the ones in power.

Looking back through church history, it seems this parade has never stopped. It marches on today, the drums as loud as they have ever been. People shout praises at Jesus, wave Jesus' banners, and identify themselves as Jesus' fans and followers. In reality, when they say they are elevating Jesus or Christianity, what's truly happening is that they have an idea of what the world ought to look like. Jesus or Christianity becomes the avatar of their aspirations.

Jesus knew this risk. He had been talking about a new kingdom the whole time, but he knew that many people, maybe most, didn't understand what he meant. Remember his words: "Not everyone who says to me, 'Lord, Lord,' will enter the kingdom of heaven, but only the one who does the will of my Father in heaven."* The streets were lined with folks shouting, "Lord, Lord," but they didn't understand what the Kingdom of Heaven brought. This scene poses an essential question for those who claim to follow Jesus. Are we following Jesus and Jesus' way? Or are we making Jesus into a sacred mascot for our team and the commitments we already have?

---

* Matthew 7:21, NRSVue.

When we shout that Jesus is Lord, are we saying we have submitted ourselves to His leadership? Or do we mean for the world to submit to us because Jesus is Lord, and we represent Jesus? When we commit to following Jesus, are we giving ourselves to the radical life of neighbor love, serving the least of these, and dying to self? Or are we simply using Jesus to bless our ideas of what culture and society ought to look like? Are we asking Jesus to give us power so we can protect ourselves from discomfort and pain?

Or are we asking Jesus to include us on his path of other-centered, co-suffering love where we give ourselves away and let Jesus save us from the unending vortex of self? This is, I think, the central and recurring question for followers of Jesus.

The people lining the streets of Jerusalem were expecting a coronation. They just didn't realize that Jesus' royal procession would be as a prisoner; his crown, bloody thorns; his throne, a cross. They certainly didn't understand that following Jesus meant walking that same path. I fear the same is still true today. Remember that it was Jesus who said, "Those who want to save their life will lose it, and those who lose their life for my sake will find it."

INWARD REFLECTION

I've mentioned a tension that exists between following Jesus' way and turning Jesus into a sacred mascot for our team. Do you see this tension within yourself? How does the desire to have God on your side as a guarantee of your security emerge in your life?

GODWARD REFLECTION

It has always been humanity's habit to imagine gods as just the biggest sort of king.* Jesus' path that led to the cross challenges that kind of thinking. Why might God need to correct our thinking?

PRAYER OF INTENTION

Write a prayer of intention around your expectations regarding whose "side" you expect God to be on. You might extend that to how (and if) you carry the label Christian and what that label means to you.

---

* Kingship is a recurring metaphor in scripture because it was written in a time when kings and emperors were the highest form of human authority. Perhaps today we need to think in other terms to convey the kind of absolute authority that this metaphor conveys.

DAY 26: DO I AVOID DISCOMFORT AT ANY COST?

John 12:20-33

REFLECTION

SOME GREEK FOLKS[*] were in Jerusalem for Passover and wanted to see Jesus. They had heard of him and tried to meet him for themselves. Their interest allowed Jesus to elaborate on something crucial for anyone seeking to follow him.

First, Jesus says a grain of wheat can never be more than a single grain unless it "falls into the earth and dies."[†] One way to understand this comment is that it explains what's coming for Jesus. Jesus, as a single seed, can only do so much. On the other hand, his death will bear much fruit, with an impact

---

[*] The Greek word used in the text here is Ἕλλην, or *the hellenes*, which might refer to people who were ethnically Greek, but more likely is referring to hellenized gentiles of some kind, people who were not Jewish and who were culturally hellenistic. People from a wide range of countries within what remained of Alexander the Great's former empire all qualified as *hellenes*.
[†] John 12:24, NRSVus.

that spreads far beyond his reach. This has proven true. Even critics and skeptics agree that Jesus' death has had an immeasurable effect on humanity. But there's another way to read these words. The gospels were written down as the first witnesses began to die, not only to record the things Jesus said and did but also to train subsequent Christians in the way of Jesus. With this audience in mind, it's not only Jesus who "falls into the earth and dies." It's also his followers.

That's the context of the next handful of statements. "Those who love their life lose it, and those who hate their life in this world will keep it for eternal life." Jesus invites his followers to prioritize their love. There is much to love in this life. Enjoy all those good things, but don't allow them to become the guiding center of life. "Whoever serves me must follow me, and where I am, there will my servant be also." Above all else, we are called to be where Jesus is.

Well, where is that? At this point in the gospel narrative, we are called to be with Jesus in carrying the cross for others. In Matthew 25, Jesus made this invitation explicit. He told us that when we serve those in need, we will find that we are serving him. He is to be found among the poor, the hungry, the naked, and the oppressed. These are not the places of power and influence. Jesus is with those on the margin of society. If we follow him, that is where we will be, too.

Getting there, though, requires a death. Remember the seed dying in the earth? Our culture and natural inclinations drive us to seek power and comfort. We are motivated to accomplish and accumulate. Why do we do this? To try, in ways big and small, to avoid dying. We want to feel safe. This is, of course, an illusion. If we strive to protect our life in these ways, we will lose it. All of us will. Dying is one of the things all humans have in common.

Following Jesus is an unfolding process where we learn

that our life's purpose isn't to avoid discomfort, holding off every kind of death and humiliation as long as possible, even at the expense of others. Instead, following Jesus' way, we die daily and rise to a life that is no longer about us. Freed from the oppressive drive to protect the self at all costs, we can now bear the fruit of love for others in practical acts of service and sacrifice.*

Like Jesus, we bear a cross, but our cross is not the nagging discomforts in our own lives. Our cross is the invitation to see those around us through other-centered, co-suffering eyes and then walk with them, even when their path includes sorrow and pain. We ensure they are not alone because we are with them. In short, we love others precisely in the same way that Jesus first loved us.

---

* Again, Heather-Bacon Shone, one of my beta readers, had a brilliant comment here: "'Dying to the world' doesn't mean 'a life of isolation and misery.' It means breaking the hold the world and its controlling humans claim on your life. That hold must be broken for your agency to burst forth. Once death is conquered, there is no further fear anyone can hold over you; no power anyone can wield. You belong to God alone."

INWARD REFLECTION

Consider the metaphor Jesus uses of a seed that falls into the ground to die. What might this metaphor mean in your present life? What might it mean for you to bear much fruit?

GODWARD REFLECTION

As you read these scripture passages, following Jesus to the cross, what do you see here about the role of comfort and discomfort in the life of faith? What does this tell you about God?

PRAYER OF INTENTION

Write a prayer of intention about your ongoing process of learning how to die to self.

DAY 27: DO I CONFUSE RELIGIOUS PRACTICE WITH A GOD-PLEASING LIFE?

Mark 11:12-23

REFLECTION

PICTURE JESUS STANDING in the busy temple court, cracking a whip. Everyone — merchants, animal handlers, money changers, and gawkers — scrambles out of his way. As the clot of merchants clears, pilgrims in the temple for the Passover season can finally see into the place of prayer. Minor functionaries stand gaping at the impudence of this country rabbi who dares interfere in the temple's workings. This is one of the most iconic scenes in Jesus' life, familiar even to those outside the church.

All four Gospels record this dramatic moment. John places it early, a sign meant to define the direction of Jesus' ministry and his relationship to the temple system. Matthew, Mark, and Luke place it after Jesus enters Jerusalem at the head of a royal procession. The Triumphal entry sealed Jesus' fate with Roman power unwilling to tolerate challengers. In the same way, the cleansing of the temple sealed Jesus' fate with the religious leadership desperate to preserve the status quo and secure its privileged position.

Both Mark's and Matthew's Gospels make an interesting literary choice.* In those two Gospels, the temple scene is placed next to a strange little interaction between Jesus and a fig tree. That's right — a fig tree. In Matthew's version, the fig tree episode happens immediately after the temple scene. In Mark, the connection is even more direct. Jesus interacts with the fig tree before and after the event, almost as if framing what happened at the temple.

On the way to the temple, Jesus passes this tree. It was in full leaf. At a distance, it seemed healthy, but closer examination showed that the fig tree had no fruit. Seeing this, Jesus spoke to the tree, "May no one ever eat from you again!" The next morning, after the temple scene, Jesus and the disciples passed this tree again. It had withered from the roots. Notice the sequence. Jesus inspected the tree for fruit. When he found none, he cursed it. It withered. Drawing from how Mark frames the temple scene in this way, some commentators suggest that Jesus' trip to the temple was a similar inspection for fruit. The temple was literally and symbolically the center of religion for Jesus' people. The daily, weekly, and annual rituals held there marked out the shape of their faith and practice. Those rituals and observances had meaning. They were important, but they were not what mattered most.

Simply put, a religion is a framework of beliefs, practices, and community. In the best case, this structure is meant to cultivate the life of the Spirit. The practices of our religion

---

* Interesting side note. This is one of the many reasons many scholars think that Matthew's Gospel used Mark as a primary source.

are meant to be formational. They ought to change us, altering how we see God, ourselves, others, and, thus, how we live in the world. However, because religion relies on visible rituals, observances, and practices, it has a nearly universal failing. This was true for the religion of Jesus' time and people — but it would be arrogant to assume this warning was meant for Judaism alone. This is a human struggle, true for every religion before or since.

If you're not connecting the dots, I'll say it directly. It is possible to perform the rituals, study and recite the teachings, participate in the culture, even love the religion itself, and not be changed. This is a crisis of epidemic scale within the modern Christian religious community. It is possible to be very religious by every observable measure and still live in ways that explicitly ignore God's instruction and contradict God's character. Even worse, it's possible to live this way while justifying oneself as a good person expressly because of all that religious activity.

When Jesus performed his fruit inspection at the temple, he was pointing out all the time, energy, and focus given to the trappings of religion, even while the heart of the religion was being violated. A fig tree with no fruit is unable to sustain a hungry soul. Jesus was not alone in this judgment. He stood in a long line of prophets before him who dramatically spoke and enacted the same message.

Consider Jeremiah, speaking for God: "Your burnt offerings are not acceptable, nor are your sacrifices pleasing to me."* Why would he say this? Because the people's "ears are closed," and they were "greedy for unjust gain." Their sacrifices brought no transformation, only self-justification. Then there's Isaiah, speaking on God's behalf: "I have had

---

* Read the whole sermon in Jeremiah 6:16-21.

enough of burnt offerings of rams and the fat of fed beasts." Even though the people were faithful in their observance of the rituals, they neglected the heart of the matter. "Everyone loves a bribe and runs after gifts. They do not defend the orphan, and the widow's cause does not come before them." If the people wanted their offerings and rituals to mean something, they needed to live differently.* One more, this time from the prophet Amos.

> I despise your festivals, and I take no delight in your solemn assemblies . . . Take away from me the noise of your songs; I will not listen to the melody of your harps. But let justice roll down like waters and righteousness like an ever-flowing stream.†

The rituals of religion can connect us to a heritage of wisdom and faith that grounds us in the turbulence of life. They can remind us of both the character of God and the life God made us for. The practices of religion, however, can also be a trap. When we do these things, we can come to see ourselves as righteous, but if those practices are not accompanied by ongoing transformation, they are a barren fig tree. Our songs, prayers, and sermons can end up being nothing more than pretty masks. We appear to be faithful people who follow God when, in the practical dealings of life, we ignore God's invitation to love and justice.

Listen to the prophets. What makes our religious practice meaningful and genuine is not the intensity of our worship, the regularity of our attendance, or the meticulous care with

---

* Isaiah's powerful message can be found in Isaiah 1:11-23.
† This passage in Amos was one that Dr. Martin Luther King called on repeatedly. Amos 5:21-24.

which we observe the rules or rituals. What makes our religious practice meaningful is when it is enlivened by a life of mercy, justice, and generosity. "What does the Lord require of you?" asked Micah, another of the ancient prophets standing in Jesus' tradition. "Do justice. Love mercy. Walk humbly with your God."* These are the fruits that let others know that the tree of our religion is healthy.

INWARD REFLECTION

How religious do you consider yourself to be? How do you come to that conclusion? What is your relationship to religious practices? This isn't a "gotcha question." I'm not asking you to rank yourself on some religiosity scale, but inviting you to consider how the practice of religion marks your life.

GODWARD REFLECTION

The strange fig tree incident says something about God's priorities for us. Reflecting on this, how do you think God relates to our various religious practices?

PRAYER OF INTENTION

Write a prayer of intention about your religious practices and their proper role in your life.

---

* Micah 6:8.

DAY 28: DOES MY ANGER FEEL VALIDATING?

John 8:1-11

REFLECTION

A GROUP of men drags a woman before Jesus, shouting that they caught her in the act of adultery. According to the law, she must be executed—stoned to death. They demand Jesus' verdict. He waits in silence. He kneels. Tension builds. He extends a finger and slowly writes in the dirt. Then Jesus stands. He says, "Let anyone among you who is without sin cast the first stone." Then, he returns his attention to the dirt. Slowly, starting with the oldest, the men slink away until no one is left but Jesus and the woman. He asks, "Woman, where are they? Is no one standing to condemn you? Then, I don't condemn you, either. Go and leave your life of sin."

Historically, this story has been called "The Woman Taken in Adultery." That title puts the spotlight in the wrong place entirely and, quite honestly, distracts us from what happened. These men intended to trap Jesus. If they could prove Jesus didn't interpret scripture correctly, they could undermine him, perhaps breaking his popularity with the people. Even better, if they caught Jesus saying something blasphemous, they could have him arrested, maybe even killed. To that end, they "took" a woman that they "caught" in the "act of adultery." I use all those scare quotes on purpose because every part of this phrase is a euphemism.

Think, for a moment, about what all this entails, exactly. The "act of adultery" usually takes place secretly and in private. Yet, here, we have a whole group of men who were oddly present at just the right time and place. Certainly, that must mean they also caught the man, but he's notably absent. Unless he's not. Is he one of the men accusing her? That would mean that instead of being an incredibly convenient opportunity (Look! A woman committing adultery! That's so helpful for our whole plot to embarrass Jesus.), the entire thing was a set-up. Some guy had lied to this woman, compromised her, and then revealed her — all as a means to an end.

If these men wanted a theological discussion with Jesus, they could have posed their question without the woman there. They used her as a prop to heighten the stakes. If Jesus agreed with the law, this woman would be killed in public, essentially on the word of Jesus. The crowd would see him acting without compassion, against his teachings, and might abandon him. On the other hand, if Jesus disagreed with the law and set the woman free, he would have publicly outed himself as a law-breaker and heretic. Good people would stop listening to him. The crowd might even turn on him and kill him for blasphemy! Either way, he wouldn't be able to save the woman. They could still put her to death for adultery. They only needed two witnesses for that. Her death would make them look righteous and Jesus look bad.

Jesus' response is of the utmost genius. A pause to slow the mob's momentum. An odd diversion to draw attention away from the terrified woman. And then a simple statement. It sounds at first like agreement. "Let the one among you who is without sin cast the first stone." Jesus didn't enter into a debate about their intention. He forced individual reflection. "Am I the one without sin? Am I willing to be part of an angry lynching mob? Will I be the one who throws the first stone?" With this quiet, individual introspection, the self-righteous momentum of the mob dissipated.

Coming together to express shared anger or grief can be a healing experience. Necessary, even. But there's a line where the shared emotional validation gives way to the rush of emotional unity that can overwhelm the individual's sense of self and morality. Being part of a self-righteous mob (even the social media kind) is easy and validating. It can quickly start to feel that anything the mob does in response to their grievance is just. What does it matter if one woman dies if we can save the whole community from the influence of this heretical teacher? What does it matter if the precipitating event was fabricated or manipulated if, in the end, we can protect our community and our way of life?

When Jesus said, "Let the one among you without sin cast the first stone," I suspect he wasn't drawing the men's attention to general human sinfulness or even to particular sins in their own past. I suspect He was talking about this very moment. The woman had been presented as a transgressor of the law worthy of death, but what of the men who had made this accusation? Were they guiltless? Had they lied and manipulated to bring this about? Had one of them participated in the adultery? Did they know their self-righteous display was a manipulative farce? Were they conscious that they were so committed to their ideology and the humiliation of their opponent that they were willing to sacrifice another human life just to prove their point? Could they see how lost they had become?

This story isn't really about the "woman taken in adultery." This story is about a group willing to justify their ideological credentials by taking the life of someone they considered to be of no value. When those men confronted Jesus, the only person he let off the hook was the woman.

INWARD REFLECTION

Have you been part of something that, in retrospect, would be fair to call an angry mob? Perhaps in a situation where the angry ones were certain they were right? What about that experience felt validating? Why? If you can't identify with that experience, perhaps you've been a victim of this kind of mob-like behavior. In either case, how did this experience shape you?

GODWARD REFLECTION

Reflect on Jesus' reaction to these men and his interaction with the woman. What does this suggest to you about God?

PRAYER OF INTENTION

Write a prayer of intention regarding your sense of how the Spirit leads you in response to this story. Are there angry groups God is inviting you to step away from? Are you sensing direction to be more brave in standing up against religious bullying like this? Is there something in Jesus' example that calls to you?

DAY 29: AM I DRAWN TO END-TIME TEACHING?

Luke 21:5-22

REFLECTION

AFTER REACHING JERUSALEM, Jesus went to the temple. In Luke's Gospel, Jesus overhears remarks about the temple's beauty and comments on its future in apocalyptic terms. This passage is one of the most dissected and debated in all the Gospels.

I grew up in a Christian denomination with tunnel vision regarding the end times. Studying timelines, prophecies, visionary beasts, and where to hide during persecution were considered essential for our spiritual preparation. It remains so for many Christians today. I understand why; the world is a painful and uncertain place. If we could look behind the curtain, wouldn't we be better prepared? And so, for centuries, people have been dredging scripture for details that line up with current events. Today, many Christians who follow one date-setter or another do not know that their particular date-setter is just one more in a long, long line.

One very early example is Hillary of Poitiers, a French Bishop, who said scripture declared the end of the world would happen in 365 CE. When that didn't happen, one of his students, Martin of Tours, pushed the date for the final battle closer to 400. He wrote the following: "There is no doubt that the anti-Christ has already been born. Firmly established already in his early years, he will, after reaching maturity, achieve supreme power." Other folks, with their own blend of scriptures and then-current events, predicted the end would happen sometime in 500 CE, or on the 6th of April 793, or in 800, or then in 847.* Later, the Black Plague was so terrible that many thought it was a sign of the end.

Some of the date-setters were fringe figures, but even well-known theologians, including Martin Luther, Jonathan Edwards, and John Wesley, set dates for the return of Christ.† The church I grew up in emerged following the date setting of William Miller, who expected Jesus' return on April 28, 1843, and then, again, March 21, 1844, and then (for sure, this time) October 22, 1844.

Why would I take up so much space recounting this dreary history? Because I want you to be clear about the temptation to certainty. Every time the calendar reaches a momentous date or geopolitical tension rises to new heights, or someone rises to power that the date-setters are sure will oppose Christianity, the charts get dusted off, and we get the name of a new Anti-Christ and a fresh date for Armageddon.

---

* Irenaus, Beatus of Liebana, Sextus Africanus, and Thiota, respectively.
† Luther said 1600. Mather said 1697 and had to revise twice before dying. Wesley thought it was going to happen in 1836. Jonathan Edwards, the famous 18th-century revivalist, was the most forward-looking, saying the end would come in 2000.

Prominent Evangelical leaders have built an industry on this cycle.* With each new prediction, the outcome is the same. Well-meaning, good-hearted people fall into a fearful frenzy as they prepare, once again, for the end of the world.

If end-time prognostication is as useless as history indicates, what do we do with this passage and others like it? Look closely. In this passage, Luke has Jesus saying, "I tell you the truth, this generation will not pass away until these things take place." He was right. In 70 CE, the Roman Legions destroyed Jerusalem and leveled the temple. One fair reading of the text is that Jesus wasn't predicting the end of days. Rather, he was warning about the end of the world he and his contemporaries were a part of, including the nation of Israel, the temple, and its religious system.† If that reading is correct, then every attempt to strip-mine this passage for clues about current events in our time must fail because the events Jesus referred to already happened.‡ If so, what

---

* If all this intrigues you this Wikipedia page has an excellent collection of end-time setters with links to original sources. https://en.wikipedia.org/wiki/List_of_dates_predicted_for_apocalyptic_events

† While this interpretation might be news to folks raised in Evangelical or Fundamentalist Christianity, it is quite old. Interpreters as far back as Eusebius (339 CE), Ambrose (396 CE), Augustine (430 CE), and Bede (735 CE) all thought that this passage referred to the destruction of Jerusalem in 70 CE. Augustine nods to the ambiguity in the text by writing, "This passage is phrased in this way in Matthew and Mark so that it is uncertain whether it is to be understood of the destruction of the city or of the end of the world . . . Luke has so arranged it that it seems to refer to the destruction of that city."

‡ Some Biblical scholars think Jesus didn't say this at all but that it was added later by editors in response to the destruction of Jerusalem in 70 CE. Some critics of this view think this is an accusation of later false additions meant to make Jesus look like he knew the future. More likely, the church community following the destruction of Jerusalem was in deep trauma, trying to make sense of what had happened, and they appropriated Jesus' words in a way that helped them make sense of what they had experienced.

spiritual fruit can we find in a passage like this? Here are some ways passages like this can be fruitful for us.

In predicting the destruction of Jerusalem, Jesus reminds us that while sacred places and practices are helpful to us, the Spirit is accessible in all places at all times. You don't need to go anywhere special or practice some ritual in just the right way—and there will be times when those places and practices won't be available to you. Do not fear; God is with you right where you are.

Jesus also warns us of the risk of losing ourselves chasing after folks who claim a special revelation. He says, quite specifically, "Do not follow them."* Our fear can make it hard for us to think clearly when a new teacher offers us certainty. This passage reminds us that fear in the face of tragic circumstances is normal. There will be wars, famines, earthquakes, plagues, even persecution. These things will happen, Jesus says, but they are not the end.† Apart from the purely natural disasters, these kinds of things are the result of living in a self-oriented, power-mad world where people (and the systems they build) are caught up in a never-ending quest for self-justification and protection and accumulation. Events like these will always happen, so long as we fail to love our neighbors as ourselves.

There are deep disagreements over how to understand apocalyptic texts in scripture. Some Christians believe Jesus will return in physical form on a visible day of judgment, in a cataclysmic event that will end this age. Other Christians, equally committed to scripture, believe these passages are symbolic. Multiple perspectives are represented in Christian

---

* Luke 21:8.
† Luke 21:9.

literature back to the second century. I expect nothing will resolve these arguments apart from seeing for ourselves.

It is most helpful to remember that the word Apocalypse doesn't refer to a cataclysmic battle between good and evil. It comes from a Greek word that means "unveiling."* What we think about the end of the world and how we relate to the predictable tragedy of human selfishness is an unveiling, revealing how we relate to uncertainty, what we think about God, and how we see other people.

---

* The English title of the last book in the Bible is "The Revelation." The title in the original Greek is ἀποκάλυψις, or *Apocalypse*. In Greek, this word literally means, "The Unveiling" or "The Revealing." What is revealed? Not secret dates and times at all, but instead, it reveals Jesus as the slain lamb who sits on the throne, a God who rules by sacrifice rather than violence, in direct subversion of the powers of Empire. If that's intriguing to you, one great book to read on the subject is *Reading Revelation Responsibly: Uncivil Worship and Witness*, by Michael Gorman.

INWARD REFLECTION

While there are many folks for whom these apocalyptic discussions are simply irrelevant, I talk regularly with those for whom these kinds of predictions produce significant anxiety. Some have even experienced these kinds of teachings as traumatic. What about you? How do you relate to Christian apocalyptic teaching? Why do you think that is?

GODWARD REFLECTION

How we relate to apocalyptic teaching and Biblical interpretation reveals who we believe God to be. Take some time and draw these connections for yourself. What does the way you relate to these passages and teachings reveal to you about the way you picture God?

PRAYER OF INTENTION

As you reflect on this topic, write a prayer of intention expressing who you sense God is inviting you to be regarding anxiety about the future.

DAY 30: IS SELF-PROTECTION MY HIGHEST GUIDING VALUE?

Mark 14:32-42

REFLECTION

IN A CRISIS, there's a point of release. Before that moment, different paths remain available. You can still affect the outcome. After this point of release, though, the choice has been made. Like a rollercoaster dropping from that first big hill, the crisis is upon you. You can only hold on until the end.

The Garden of Gethsemane is that point for Jesus. The pressure is building. Judas has already gone to get Jesus' enemies. Jesus only has a few more minutes to make choices that alter his future circumstances. He could call together all his followers in Jerusalem and make a show of force, or, if he hurries, he could leave town and get to safety. Maybe he could do something supernatural. In this moment, what does Jesus choose? He sits in the pressure, feeling the sorrow, perhaps even the fear. He asks his friends to stay with him. He prays that he doesn't want to go through with it.

Early Christians, as they began to discuss and write about their experience of Jesus, noted two apparently contradictory things. They had experienced Jesus as a normal human person — subject to hunger and pain, limited in capacity and knowledge. But they also experienced in Jesus an unprecedented sense of the Divine presence. They saw Jesus do and say things that, in their understanding, only God could do.*

In the vulnerability of the Garden of Gethsemane, we are given access to Jesus' intimate and interior struggle. Jesus, the human man, says, "I don't want to go through this. Take this cup away!" That's a normal, natural response to pain. Our desire to survive and thrive causes us to recoil from threats to our safety. We were made for life! Yet, the path of pain that lies ahead for Jesus serves others. His pain will change everything. While reacting to the anticipation of pain, he also accepts and trusts. Human nature and ego say, "We must protect ourselves at any cost." The Divine nature always acts in love, so Jesus can say, "This isn't what I want for myself right now, but it is what serves the good of all."

In this scene, we can see the tension inherent in the Incarnation. The human drive to survive and avoid pain is normal, and Jesus is fully human. The response of other-centered co-suffering love, which calls us to enter into pain

---

* The question of whether all early Christians saw Jesus as fully Divine and fully human is an interesting and complicated one. It's a question that led to three hundred years of controversy about the nature of Christ. Still today, while most Christians accept the Nicene doctrine of the full Divinity of Jesus, there are numerous understandings and shades of interpretation. Unpacking this is far too much to be handled here. For the purpose of this devotional, I am acknowledging both sides of this discussion. Jesus was fully human, which means that he had real human emotions and mental states, like fear and uncertainty. Jesus was fully Divine. At the very least, this means he had unprecedented, experiential, subjective access to the Spirit of God.

and perhaps even death, is Divine. Both of these motives are fully present in the garden. Ultimately, Jesus chooses the path of acceptance rather than self-protection.

With that choice, the garden becomes the site of Jesus' death — not because that's where he was crucified but because that is where he confirmed his commitment to this painful path. In classical Christian language, we talk about this as the moment of Jesus' complete surrender to the will of the Father. In the language of psychology, we could also talk about this as the moment of ego death.

You and I are not Jesus. We aren't called to the cross to die for humanity, but even so, we aren't strangers to Gethsemane. In small ways, over and over, we come into the garden feeling the pressure, grief, and pain of a decision that has consequences for us and those we love. Two powerful motives threaten to pull us apart: Our natural human desire to avoid discomfort, pain, and death, on the one hand; the mark of the Divine in us, a love for others that is willing to suffer in order to serve, on the other. Our ego demands acknowledgment, pressing us to power up, prove we're right, strike back, move to higher ground, and do whatever we can to change the circumstances to avoid the pain. The image of God within us and the Spirit moving on our hearts invites us to resist the ego's demands. Whenever we choose other-centered, co-suffering love, it's a little death for the ego.*

The garden comes for all of us, over and over again. Occasionally, it comes with big, life-changing decisions that

---

* **An important note for those in abusive or toxic relationships**: The inner drive to make destructive self-injuring choices for those who are abusing us doesn't come from God. Someone telling you it is the right, moral, or Godly thing to stay in relationships or situations where you are being abused is manipulating you and doesn't have your best interest in mind. You are allowed to leave abusive situations.

have painful consequences for everyone involved. Sometimes, it comes with small, daily choices that impact the future. In those moments, we feel profoundly alone as we wrestle with the competing drives of self-protection and ego death. Recall this scene when you find yourself in a garden of a painful decision. Jesus walked this path, too. That means God knows from personal experience how the garden feels. Unlike Jesus, whose sleeping friends couldn't understand what he was going through, you are accompanied by One who's been there.

The ego never wants to die, but most of the time, we find more life and deeper love on the other side of that painful death.

INWARD REFLECTION

In what ways is self-protection a driving motivation for you? Are there times you can remember when your desire to protect yourself led you to act in ways that weren't loving? Are there times, looking back, when you wish you had chosen a more painful but also more loving path?

GODWARD REFLECTION

If Jesus reflects the heart of God, what do Jesus' experience and choices in the garden show you about God?

PRAYER OF INTENTION

Write a prayer of intention about your struggle with the death of ego and elevating self-preservation above love.

DAY 31: DOES THE GOODNESS OF MY CAUSE JUSTIFY COERCION?

Mark 14:43-46

REFLECTION

IN POPULAR CULTURE, the name Judas has come to mean "betrayer," the turn-coat friend who betrays those he loves. This short passage shows how that name took on this meaning. Judas, who had been one of the twelve disciples, one of those who walked closely with Jesus, enters the garden at the head of a band of armed men. He kisses Jesus — the planned sign — and the armed men take Jesus into custody.

Most know Jesus' enemies paid Judas to turn him over. It's easy to assume Judas' motivation was greed, but that may not be the whole story. After Jesus' arrest and trial, Judas tried to return the money. When those who paid him off wouldn't take it back, he killed himself. I suspect Judas wasn't in it for the money. More likely, he was in it for the revolution.

Many scholars think the text indicates Judas was a Zealot. The Zealots were an extremist faction that engaged in violence to overthrow the Roman occupation. The disciples expected Jesus to rise to power in Jerusalem, fulfilling their Messianic dreams. Perhaps Judas was depending on more than hope, expecting an inciting incident to pressure Jesus to act. If Jesus was threatened, it might rally the people. Judea was a smoldering bed of political frustration and anger, ready to ignite with the right spark. If so, Judas was willing to take the bribe if he could create the circumstance where Jesus would begin the violent overthrow of Jerusalem's puppet leaders. Heck, those leaders would be paying for their own downfall! He didn't expect Jesus to be tortured and killed. When he saw that Jesus wasn't going to fight back, Judas was undone with remorse.

I suspect that Judas loved Jesus. I think he was hopeful Jesus would bring about a new order of things, righting wrongs and making life better for his people. To be fair, expectations like this were supported by ancient prophecies that promised the Messiah would bring deliverance to prisoners and liberate the oppressed.* But if Judas was thinking along these lines, he was terribly wrong about how Jesus would fulfill these promises. I suspect Judas saw Jesus' popularity, his ability to heal and provide food, and his charismatic teaching as assets for a regime change project rather than signs of Jesus' new way of life. He may have loved Jesus, but he certainly loved his vision of the world more.

Judas' vision, however, was faulty. He had not understood Jesus' way of love. He still believed the only way to get things done was through manipulation, coercion, and violence. A short, bloody transition would clear the way for the new, peaceful kingdom. This betrayal wasn't just of Jesus as a friend but also of Jesus' way. Hatred can't evoke love.

---

* For example, see Isaiah 61.

Vengeance will never bring about forgiveness and reconciliation. Violence is unable to establish lasting peace.

Jesus' followers today face the grave temptation to follow in Judas' steps. In many ways, big and small, we are tempted to use Jesus to further our own ends. We can come to believe that our party, our group, our church is right, and that means we are justified to push our goals forward at any cost. We think ourselves wise and pragmatic as we leverage the tools of coercion and even violence to establish Jesus' kingdom on earth.

This is Judas' trap. For Jesus, the ends never justified the means. The means are the end in the process of becoming. Other-centered, co-suffering love is the means, bringing about an end wholly in alignment with God's nature. Judas wanted to force an outcome on a timeline that made sense to him, but God — and love — cannot be forced. The new kingdom way will only come through the long, slow path of other-centered, co-suffering love.

INWARD REFLECTION

Can you relate to the idea of being so certain in the goodness of your cause that you were willing to manipulate or coerce others toward your goals? Why do you think this temptation is so common and so powerful?

GODWARD REFLECTION

The fact that Jesus welcomed Judas has something to tell us about God's nature. What do you see in the story of Judas that shows you something about God?

PRAYER OF INTENTION

Write a prayer of intention around your temptations to use manipulation or coercion to bring about the good results you're so certain are best.

DAY 32: CAN I ACT WITH RESTRAINT WHEN FALSELY ACCUSED?

Matthew 26:57-68

REFLECTION

AFTER THE SOLDIERS arrested Jesus in the garden, they took him to the house of the high priest, where he was tried before the Sanhedrin. If you crossed the Senate with the Supreme Court, but all the members were influential pastors and religious studies professors, you'd have a pretty good sense of what the Sanhedrin was like. Some of these judges already had an outcome in mind. They were going to convict Jesus of a capital crime so they would have a legal basis to have him killed. That would solve the problem of his growing influence that disturbed their position and power.

They wanted the trial to look proper. They had witnesses lined up to give false testimony, but their law required two witnesses to agree, and none of them did. In the end, it was Jesus' own words that convicted him. The high priest asked if Jesus was "the Messiah, the Son of God." Jesus responded,

"You have said so, but I tell you, 'From now on you will see the Son of Man seated at the right hand of Power and coming on the clouds of heaven.'"*

With these words, Jesus referenced scripture most in that room would have been familiar with from the ancient book of Daniel:

> In my vision at night I looked, and there before me was one like a son of man, coming with the clouds of heaven. He approached the Ancient of Days and was led into his presence. He was given authority, glory and sovereign power . . . and his kingdom is one that will never be destroyed.†

That did the trick. Blasphemy was a capital crime, and those words from Jesus were heard as a direct claim of divinity. Jesus said the words in front of the Sanhedrin, meaning they could all stand as witnesses. Done and done.

At this moment, the paradox of power shows itself. The Sanhedrin had all the power. They could make decisions of life and death. And yet, with all their resources, they couldn't convict Jesus. He was only convicted because he chose to give them what they needed. Who was really in control?

Jesus cited an apocalyptic text that portrayed God granting all power and dominion to "one like a son of man," who had ascended through the clouds from earth to stand before God. He was claiming this power for himself. Yet, Jesus didn't seem to have that kind of power as he stood before his judges. Was he out of his mind? Think about what happens after this. Jesus is beaten, dragged before the Roman governor to finalize the death sentence, tortured, and

---

* Matthew 26:64-64, NRSVue.
† Daniel 7:13-14, NIV.

crucified. Either he didn't have the power he thought he had, or Divine power is about something besides control.

We're so used to people scrambling for power and control, chasing it through every possible means—influence, celebrity, wealth, platform, followers, politics, and after we can't get our way any other way, the ability to leverage violence to get what we want. We want to be in control, make sure bad things can't happen to us, and manage the narrative. We want our team in charge. Human history is just a parade of names we remember because of their role in the never-ending quest for control. Even Christians fall into this. Only our pursuit of power gets justified under the banner of building Christ's kingdom.* Because we consider this the ultimate good, we think we can justify any means to get there. In this way, we pervert Christ's mission and become one more group building a self-serving empire.

Watching Jesus stand before the Sanhedrin ought to challenge our view of things. The one who has real power in this scene is Jesus. He chooses the path of self-sacrifice. He has the highest possible authority yet doesn't defend his reputation or provide a shocking rebuttal to his accusers. Jesus doesn't leverage his popularity, calling people to assemble in his defense. He doesn't use miraculous abilities to prove his identity or stop those attacking him. He does nothing that registers as powerful by human standards.

To follow Jesus means more than accepting certain claims about him as truth. It also (perhaps more importantly) means we follow in his footsteps. This may not be very comforting to consider, but the way of Jesus is the path that leads away

---

* An unfortunate turn of phrase that contributes to our misdirection. Jesus already established his kingdom, and is inviting us to live as if we are part of it. We aren't building anything for God; God is working in, around, and through all of us, and we can be part of this reconciling work if we are willing.

from the pursuit of control and coercive power. Once we get this, it must change how we relate to the conflicts in our lives, especially when we face unfair accusations.

INWARD REFLECTION

How do you react when others falsely accuse you, particularly when you have the power or position to do something about it? Why do you think this is?

GODWARD REFLECTION

However we understand Jesus' nature, this scene is worth pausing over. If Jesus stood in the Sanhedrin as an ordinary human man, his acceptance and equanimity are worth reflecting on. If Jesus stood there in conscious possession of Divine power, his purposeful restraint is instructive. If Jesus provides a window into the nature of God, what might this scene say about who God is and what God is up to?

PRAYER OF INTENTION

Are there areas in your life where you sense God might be inviting you to purposeful restraint? Write a prayer of intention about this.

DAY 33: DO I HOLD MYSELF WITH CONDEMNATION OR COMPASSION?

Matthew 26:69-75

REFLECTION

IN THE GARDEN, when the armed men came, Peter jumped to Jesus' defense. When Jesus was led away, Peter followed. Maybe he wanted to stay close enough to see what happened. Perhaps he hoped he could intervene in some way. Not long before this, Peter had made a vow that he would never—under any circumstances—abandon Jesus.*

But then Peter found himself in a courtyard outside the trial, surrounded by folks he thought were his enemies. That's when a servant asked Peter if he was with Jesus. His accent gave him away. Peter denied. Others by the fire picked up the accusation. Peter denied again. The challenger grew more confident. Peter swore. The rooster crowed.

I relate so deeply to Peter. I've made grave declarations of

---

* See Matthew 26:35.

commitment, promises to stick with someone, be a warrior for a cause, or give my all. Those promises seemed right at the time, even righteous, but I could not see how far beyond my capacity they were. In my certainty, I couldn't even see how my motives were mixed. Zeal and lack of self-awareness put me in a position where I would inevitably fall short, fail, and even betray. The scripture ends simply: "He went out and wept bitterly." I've been there. Being human means overstepping. We often say things we haven't carefully considered. Then we let people down, even people we love or thought to help. This is painfully true of me. Has it been true for you? I expect so.

Knowing the fragility of our intentions and the frequency with which we fail, you might think we'd relate to ourselves and others with compassion. Yet, many of us don't. We live with a gavel of judgment hanging over our heads. Whether we're trying to live up to the expectations of our parents, our religious community, or our ideas of what it means to be a good person, it can feel like our words and actions become evidence in a trial against us. Did we fail to live up to our expectations? Did we overstep and commit more than we can fulfill? Did we end up hurting someone we love? Some of us have, and we've found ourselves mired in self-condemnation.[*]

When we relate to ourselves first with condemnation, it can easily color how we perceive others. Some of us come to

---

[*] To be exceedingly clear: when we hurt someone else, our first concern shouldn't be whether or not we're being compassionate with ourselves. Our first concern ought to be making things right — confessing, apologizing, repairing. The other-centered, co-suffering way of Jesus calls us, when and where we are able, to make things right with those we've hurt. The issue in view in this entry is separate from this. When we carry ongoing shame and condemnation for ourselves, Jesus' restoration of Peter can offer us hope that God wants to bring us out of that dark place, so that we can relate to ourselves and others with compassion.

measure those around us with the same cynical eye, evaluating every word for intent, looking for malice. When we find it or even suspect it might be there, we leap to judgment. We're tempted to hear the declarations of others in the worst possible light. (This is especially true when the other person is someone we already disagree with.) Measuring each statement or action in this way has consequences. In relationships with others, it leads to judgment, alienation, and exclusion. In our relationships with ourselves, it leads to shame. In our relationship with God, it leads to separation and fear.

This episode of scripture is often called Peter's denial of Christ. That makes sense because he denied his relationship with Jesus, but that word runs deeper. When Peter made those declarations of loyalty, he was denying his humanity, weakness, and the uncertainty of life. He was denying his inability to control the outcome of circumstances, even those that involved him! When he cursed and swore to disclaim connection to Jesus, he was denying his own heart and precious relationship with a friend. He was even in denial about Jesus' prediction of these terrible events.

After the crucifixion and resurrection, Jesus forgave and reinstated Peter. On the beach of the Sea of Galilee, Jesus released Peter from his shame and helped him emerge from denial.* With his loving forgiveness and guidance, Jesus can do the same for us. Even so, it might serve us to keep Peter in mind. Maybe we should be a bit more mindful of our limitations when we make righteous declarations and less judgmental of the limitations and overstatements of others.

---

* If you're not familiar with this part of the story, you can read this moving scene in John 21.

INWARD REFLECTION

Would you say you primarily relate to yourself from a place of compassion or condemnation? Why do you think this is?

GODWARD REFLECTION

It's fascinating that the early Christians chose to keep Peter's denial as a sacred story. Because he was an influential leader after Jesus, you might expect a more sanitized version to be told in the church's early years. How might including this story of failure within scripture inform how you think of God?

PRAYER OF INTENTION

Consider the roles of condemnation and shame in your life, in how you see yourself, God, and others. Write a prayer of intention about who you want to be in this regard.

DAY 34: AM I WILLING TO PURSUE PEACE?

Luke 23:13-25

REFLECTION

THE RELIGIOUS LEADERS finally convicted Jesus. The sentence was death. Because Israel was an occupied territory of the Roman Empire, they had no authority to carry out this sentence. So, they dragged Jesus to the Roman Proconsul, Marcus Pontius Pilatus. The Gospels call him Pilate.

After a brief interview, Pilate decided the prisoner wasn't worthy of death. Pilate thought to solve his impasse with the leaders demanding execution through his tradition of the Passover Clemency. Once a year, at Passover, Pilate released one prisoner to show Rome's benevolence. He would do as he always did, but this time, he would let the people choose. There was another death row prisoner called Barabbas. Perhaps Pilate thought that the choice between the two was so stark that Jesus would be set free. When offered the option, though, the crowd demanded Barabbas instead of

Jesus. Surprised, Pilate gave in to the crowd's demands, signing Jesus' death warrant.

Who was this substitute? John's Gospel identifies Barabbas as a robber, but Matthew's Gospel identifies him as a murderer and insurrectionist. There's even some early textual evidence that his name might have been Jesus Barabbas.* Was Barabbas on death row, not just for murder, but also because he had been an active participant in a violent protest against Rome's occupation? There's even an intriguing possibility that this name carried a Messianic association.†

Who would the people choose? Would they pick the preacher calling them to forgive their enemies and find peace through reconciliation? Or would they choose the violent revolutionary, who had already shown a willingness to kill for liberation? This is the choice Pilate offered the crowd — and it seems like Pilate didn't understand the crowd as well as he thought.

We're still faced with this same choice today. Choosing the path of violent power only seems pragmatic in our world of conflict. It's the realistic option. We have to protect

---

* The oldest reference that supports this is in a 3rd century text. Scholars are divided about whether Matthew's original text included this full name and it was later removed out of reverence for Jesus, or whether it was added in later, as a copyist error. All the evidence and arguments are laid out in a paper called "Jesus Barabbas, A Nominal Messiah?" By Robert Moses. A more accessible treatment, that ultimately comes down on the side of this being a copyist error, can be read here: https://tyndalehouse.com/explore/articles/jesus-barabbas-or-jesus-christ/

† Brian Zahnd drew my attention to this interesting point, which led to a fun afternoon of historical research. The Greek name Βαραββᾶς, or *Barabbas*, is a transliteration of an Aramaic name, בַּר־אַבָּא, which is made from two words: *bar*, son of, and *abba*, father. Some scholars think that this is more likely a title or perhaps a reference to this man's father rather than a given name. If the name meant "Son of the Father," it could also have been a Messianic reference.

ourselves, don't we? The best defense is a great offense. So, we keep the peace by continually increasing our capacity to wage war and hoping that a punitive carceral system will end crime. We believe we can achieve the peaceful world we long for by doing whatever is necessary to keep our "team" in power. Power is the way to peace. Isn't that what human history teaches us? This reasoning makes sense to many. It causes one of the most serious points of tension people have with the way of Jesus. In following Jesus, we are being asked to set aside the tools of power and violence — even though they seem to work!

Many modern Christians are not aware that for the first four hundred years of the church, many Christian theologians were explicitly anti-violence. Justin Martyr, writing in the 2nd century, said:

> We have exchanged our swords for plowshares, our spears for farm tools . . . now we cultivate the fear of God, justice, kindness, faith, and the expectation of the future given us through the Crucified One.[*]

In the late 2nd century, Tertullian wrote, "It is absolutely forbidden to repay evil with evil."[†] Athanasius, one of the most influential early theologians, writing in the 3rd century, said, "Christians, instead of arming themselves with swords, extend their hands in prayer."[‡] In many areas of the church during this period, Christians refused military duty and often paid a great price for doing so. Origen, a North African theologian, wrote in the early 3rd century, "You cannot

---

[*] Justin Martyr, *Dialogue with Trypho*, 109f.
[†] Tertullian, *On Patience*, 3.
[‡] Athenasius, *On the Incarnation*, 8.52.

demand military service of Christians any more than you can of priests. We do not go forth as soldiers with the Emperor, even if he demands this."* In response to a query about whether soldiers could become Christian, Tertullian commented, "Christ, in disarming Peter, disarmed every soldier."†

It was only later, starting in the late 4th century, when Christianity became the official religion of the Roman Empire, that theologians began to talk about "just war" and the possibility of such a thing as Christian violence. Even after this view came to prominence, a solid minority voice has remained throughout history, reminding us that Jesus resisted violence to serve his cause at every opportunity.‡

On the steps of Pilate's palace, two men stood: One, a peaceful teacher who invited others to a new life marked by other-centered, co-suffering love — the other, a likely revolutionary who attempted to bring freedom through violence. The crowd was invited to choose. At that moment, and in so many moments since, the crowd picked the path of expediency and the long-standing human dream of peace through retributive violence. The way of Jesus challenges us to choose the harder path.

---

* Origen, *Against Celsus*, 8.73.
† Tertullian, *Apology*, 37.
‡ If you're interested in learning more, you can learn about the varying applications of Christian non-violence by researching the Anabaptist movement and modern "peace churches." A good starting point is *A Field Guide to Christian Nonviolence*, by Cramer and Werntz.

INWARD REFLECTION

It's likely that everyone in that crowd wanted freedom and peace for their country and families. They just wanted to see the Roman occupiers leave their land. The desire to make things happen by force is natural. Do you ever find that you want to force things forward? How do you feel about the use of power and violence to accomplish what you consider to be good ends?

GODWARD REFLECTION

Some have imagined a different version of these events where, instead of Jesus meekly proceeding to his death, he overwhelmed his opponents by demonstrating his strength. That is not, however, what the gospel presents. As you reflect on this sequence of events, what do you see about the nature of God?

PRAYER OF INTENTION

Reflect on your own views toward violence, even violence considered righteous or just, then write a prayer of intention that encapsulates how you sense God is leading you.

DAY 35: DO I POWER UP WHEN CHALLENGED?

Mark 15:15-20

REFLECTION

PILATE GAVE in to the crowd's demands. He released Barabbas and handed Jesus over to the soldiers, who would execute the death sentence. Full of their power over and contempt for the Jewish people, these soldiers acted out a hideous role-play. Every part of their game was a twisted mockery of respect due to a king—a royal robe, a crown, a scepter, even sarcastic displays of homage, followed by a parody of a royal procession.

This is more than mere cruelty toward someone these soldiers considered powerless and likely crazy. More likely, this was a visceral reaction to Jesus' claim to kingship, a humiliating show meant to demonstrate exactly how little power he had. Jesus would get crowned, all right. Roman soldiers knew about due deference. They'd give Jesus precisely the homage they thought he deserved. He would see—and all his followers would see — that no one can stand against the power of the empire!

This is how coercive power behaves. Whether vested in an empire, an economic system, or a church board, power is most offended by that which challenges its sovereignty. Don't believe me? Then, suggest out loud that America isn't a righteous country, that unregulated free-market capitalism requires exploitation to function, or that your church denomination has a problem with power and abuse. Say these things in the wrong company, and watch the fireworks.

If these statements were not, to some extent, true, there would be no emotional basis for such defensiveness. When the system we are invested in is challenged, we feel attacked. It gets under our skin when someone suggests they have a higher claim to our loyalty. When the threat is too strong, this defensiveness can erupt in violence to indisputably make clear who really is the strong one around here. The same move to dominate can be seen in some parents, bosses, boards, and even church organizations.

The supreme irony is that the Roman soldiers thought they were showing Jesus' claim to be empty when, in fact, they validated everything he had said. Their angry scorn demonstrated the superiority of gracious humility. Their vengeance illuminated the brittle pretension of human power. Their hatred revealed the nobility of neighbor love. These soldiers were acting as if they were gods, and in doing so, proved that they knew nothing of God. They were children of wrath, born into a system shaped by wrath, enacting wrath as a means of self-justification.*

---

* My beta readers and I had an energetic conversation about this paragraph. If it raises your eyebrow, consider this: I am not suggesting the soldiers were "children of wrath" because they tortured Jesus. I am saying they were born into a system of domination and coercion, and their entire understanding of

In the face of Jesus' claims to lordship, all others who consider themselves lords must either bow in acknowledgment or fight back to protect their illegitimate claim. Their violent reaction to Jesus shows exactly why other-centered, co-suffering love is necessary for humanity. What else can save us from the cycle of violence needed to prop up the lies of power and self-justification?

Jesus invites us to leave all of that behind and follow. He calls us to turn the other cheek and walk the extra mile.* He invites us to pay attention to the small and unimportant, warning us not to become enamored of the influential and powerful. Jesus tells us to love our neighbor as ourselves and to do unto others as we would have them do unto us. He commands us to love others as He has loved us. This is his sovereign command, which defines the nature of life under his lordship. His way challenges our sense of sovereignty, not because he has dominated us and forced us to his will, but because his loving invitation exposes selfish domination for the evil it is. His way saves us from self-destruction and opens the door to reconciliation, restoration, and new life.

---

the world and their relationship to it was enculturated by this system. Like all children, they were acting out the patterns of the system that shaped them.

* **Important Note:** My editor and several beta readers asked asked, "How does one differentiate abuse from turning the other cheek?" My short answer to anyone in an abusive situation is this: Despite what you may have heard, you are permitted to leave and you should. My longer answer is that abusing others deforms the soul. If I am living from a place of other-centered, co-suffering love, then I can't allow an abuser to continue on their path, because to do so would be to enable what is causing soul damage. If I am able to intervene in abuse, I should, not only for the victim (who is my first priority) but also for the abuser.

INWARD REFLECTION

Have you ever experienced the temptation to power up or attempt to dominate in order to defend your sense of being right? Or maybe you've experienced someone else doing this at your expense. What was your experience like? How did it impact you?

GODWARD REFLECTION

In the Passion Week story, Jesus' experience and behavior look nothing like what we expect from powerful people. It's possible to see these events as a tragedy, yet the early Christians came to see them as revealing God's glory. What might the events in today's reading show you about God?

PRAYER OF INTENTION

The contrast between the brutal power of Rome and the powerful love of Jesus invites us to consider our relationship to power, especially when Jesus' way runs counter to the comfortable tendencies of our own culture. Write a prayer of intention that encompasses your sense of Jesus' invitation to you on this subject.

DAY 36: AM I DYING WITH JESUS?

John 19:13-17

REFLECTION

AFTER SCOURGING and staging their brutal mocking coronation, the soldiers handed Jesus over to the executioners. They threw the cross-beam on his shoulders and led him to the site of public executions, a hill outside the city called Golgotha, the "place of the Skull." Jesus' followers shouldn't have been surprised. He gave them ample warning. Now, it was happening. The idea of Jesus' death was so far outside their preconception that when Jesus said it, they couldn't hear him. They imagined he was mistaken or maybe just speaking in metaphors. This was no metaphor. Jesus was carrying his cross through the city to the place of death.

All these years later, people who follow Jesus often make the same mistake the first disciples made, even though we have so much more information. We've read the gospels. We know the passion story. Crucifixes and paintings of the crucifixion are common enough. If we've been around church for any length of time, we have some idea about what crucifixion means. And still, we think Jesus wasn't being serious, at least where we are concerned.

In Luke's Gospel, Jesus told his followers,

> The Son of Man must undergo great suffering and be rejected by the elders, chief priests, and scribes and be killed and on the third day be raised." Then he said to them all, "If any wish to come after me, let them deny themselves and take up their cross daily and follow me.*

The invitation to take up our cross daily is at the heart of Jesus' way. This saying of Jesus has given birth to countless sermons and songs, but when we talk about "bearing our cross," what do we really think Jesus meant?

Many times, when we talk about "carrying our cross," we often mean putting up with some inconvenience or discomfort, maybe a personality tick, an annoying relative, or perhaps a delay in our plans. Much less frequently, we're referring to some unavoidable suffering. But Jesus wasn't talking about irritations or delays in our happiness. He was talking about death. For Jesus, for every person in his original audience, and for Christians until the 4th century when crucifixion was abolished in the Roman Empire, the cross was an instrument of torture and death. When Jesus told his followers they would be called on to "take up their cross daily," he was inviting them to come and die.†

---

* Luke 9:22-23, NRSVue.
† Dietrich Bonhoeffer, the Lutheran pastor and theologian known for his opposition to the Nazis and his execution in an internment camp, expressed strong opinions about this: "The cross is laid on every Christian. The first Christ-suffering which every man must experience is the call to abandon the

Undoubtedly, the call to die daily can't refer to literal death every day for every person. Necessarily, we must also understand this as a spiritual metaphor. Yet, perhaps we ought to delay our rush to move from the literal to the symbolic. If we're not thinking carefully about this, the turn to metaphor can transmute Jesus' invitation into something meaningless.

For some followers of Jesus, through history and even today, this call was indeed a call to literal death. Christians would die for their faith, for their association with the faithful, and often for the way their faith led them to resist the powerful. Sometimes, they would die because of prejudice. In times of persecution, Christians would often die because some angry or jealous neighbor turned them in to the authorities. In the first century, Christians would die because in their unwillingness to offer incense to the emperor, they were considered obstinate and disrespectful. This hasn't stopped in modern times. Just one example: In the eighties, Salvadorean Christians would die for speaking out against the government's use of Death Squads to consolidate power. It has always been the case that following Jesus carries the possibility of being a literal death sentence.

For others, perhaps most, the invitation to take up the cross daily isn't literal. We must begin to look to the metaphor for meaning, especially those of us who live with some level of comfort or privilege. But as we do, be careful

---

attachments of this world . . . Thus it begins; the cross is not the terrible end to an otherwise god-fearing and happy life, but it meets us at the beginning of our communion with Christ. When Christ calls a man, He bids him come and die. It may be a death like that of the first disciples who had to leave home and work to follow Him, or it may be a death like Luther's, who had to leave the monastery and go out into the world. But it is the same death every time — death in Jesus Christ, the death of the old man at his call." Bonhoeffer, *The Cost of Discipleship* (London: SCM Press, 1948) 44.

not to let the cross lose its edge. To understand this invitation to a daily cross, let Jesus' cross guide us. What was the cross for Jesus? It was death on behalf of others. The cross was the final act of other-centered, co-suffering love in Jesus' earthly life. It wasn't a mild inconvenience delaying his plans. The cross was Jesus laying down his life for his friends. And for his enemies.

If Jesus' literal cross is a model for our metaphorical one, this invitation must refer to the process of dying to self when we serve others at a cost. We die an ego-death when we are willing to be wrong or weak or let go of defending our reputation. We die an ego-death when we share what we have with others, even when we're not sure we want to. When we stand with those who are suffering, or are marginalized, or are being dehumanized, we begin to walk the way of the cross. When we refuse to go along with the machinery of power and its inevitable exploitation, when we transgress our culture's expectations of self-justification, self-protection, and self-aggrandizement, the shadow of the cross falls across our lives.

Some theologians have taken to calling this the Cruciform life. That just means that the kind of life Jesus' followers live is shaped like the cross. Love for God and love for neighbor flow together, each expressing and strengthening the other. Ego kneels, allowing this love to become embodied in acts of other-centered, burden-bearing, co-suffering love.

What might feel like death turns out to be resurrection, enabling us to trust more and more that the cross really is the path of life. Then, we discover we have become participants in God's work to reconcile and restore the world. Take up your cross. This way is life.

INWARD REFLECTION

If you grew up in a church context, what did the phrase "take up your cross" mean to you? If you didn't, what imagery comes to mind as you think about this phrase?

GODWARD REFLECTION

Some Christian theological streams primarily discuss the cross as something Jesus did for us. It was Jesus' experience, done as part of God's plan for salvation. In some of those narratives, our role is simply to accept that Jesus did this for us. While there is some truth to this way of seeing the cross, Jesus' words imply a more direct experience: "If any wish to come after me, let them deny themselves and take up their cross daily and follow me.'" What does this tell you about God's work in us and the world?

PRAYER OF INTENTION

Reflect on Jesus' invitation to take up your cross, and write a prayer of intention about what this means to you.

DAY 37: AM I A WILLING BURDEN-BEARER?

Mark 15:21

REFLECTION

AS THE ROMAN soldiers led Jesus out to the place of execution, he was forced to carry the crossbeam himself. He was already severely injured and exhausted. The wood was heavy; he was weak. The soldiers, perhaps frustrated by Jesus' slow staggering, pressed a passer-by into service. Mark's Gospel captures this moment in a single verse that offers a fascinating window into the life of the early church.

> They compelled a passer-by, who was coming in from the country, to carry his cross; it was Simon of Cyrene, the father of Alexander and Rufus.*

Why would the gospel writer know this stranger's name?

---
* Mark 15:21, NRSVue.

Why would he know the names of his children? Why would he include them here? All three Synoptic Gospels* mention Simon of Cyrene, but only Mark mentions his sons. Mark's Gospel is most likely the earliest gospel account. A good argument can be made for it being written between 64-76 CE. Simon was a random stranger in the crowd. How could Mark have known his name? Simon very likely had already died by the time the Gospel was written.

I suspect the reason is simple. Mark knew Simon and his sons' names because, before the Gospel was written, they had become part of the early community of Christians. Simon was from Cyrene, a city in northern Africa, in the region of modern-day Libya. He was likely in Jerusalem for Passover, one of the many pilgrims who made their way there each year. Their inclusion in Mark's narrative likely means that at some point after that fateful day, Simon and his family became followers of Jesus and so were known in the community.

In Paul's letter to the Romans, he greets a leader in the Roman church named Rufus.† Is it possible that this is the boy mentioned by Mark, all grown up? Polycarp, a disciple of John who taught and wrote a generation later, also cites a Rufus, who was known to work among the apostles.‡ While

---

* Matthew, Mark, and Luke are referred to as the Synoptics, which means "same vision." This name came into being as scholars noticed how many stories these three Gospels share and even how often they use the same words. Modern scholars propose this is because of shared use of sources, either Matthew and Luke both used Mark as a source, or perhaps all three Gospels used a source that no longer exists. Regardless of how this similarity came to be, Matthew and Mark are remarkably similar, and Luke shares quite a bit with them. John, on the other hand, is significantly different in which stories are told, in which sequence those stories happen, and in the language used.

† Romans 16:13.

‡ Polycarp is one of the earliest Christian theologians following the apostolic era whose writing we still have and can be historically verified. He

we can't say with certainty if these mentions of Rufus refer to the same person, it offers an intriguing possibility. If Simon of Cyrene became a follower of Jesus, and his sons Alexander and Rufus subsequently became leaders in the early church, it would make sense that the gospel writers knew Simon's name. It also means that in this call out, Mark points his readers to first-hand witnesses of the crucifixion, men who would still have been alive and accessible to the community.

I suspect, however, that this name drop is more than a citation of eyewitnesses. Simon of Cyrene carried Jesus' cross. If he became a follower of Jesus, imagine the significance. Remember Jesus' words we reflected on in the last reading? Simon of Cyrene was one among them who had literally taken up the cross and done so in a situation where he had little choice. He was a living parable.

"Remember Simon," the Christians in the early church might have said. "There are times when you will have no choice. Life will press you into service. You will be the one present and able to bear up under the burden of others. It may come at a cost to you. It may be terrifying. Even so, God will appoint you to walk a ways carrying the cross of another. When you do that, you are not only serving them but also joining Jesus in his passion." Paul taught this principle when he said that we are to "bear one another's burdens and so fulfill the law of Christ."*

It may seem odd to modern people, but the early

---

was born about 35 years after the crucifixion, and died in 155 CE. As a young leader, he was ultimately appointed to be the bishop of the church in Smyrna, the modern day city of Izma in Turkey. Polycarp and his friend, Papias, are attested as having been taught by the Apostle John. Polycarp mentions Rufus in his epistle to the Philippians, a letter of pastoral instruction written in the 2nd century.

* Galatians 6:2.

Christians did not see their faith as a way to some future, better life. Neither did they consider Christianity a means for personal growth. Their faith in Jesus meant accepting the invitation to carry Jesus' cross. "As I have loved you, so you should love each other," Jesus said. This meant far more than familial affection. They understood that Jesus' love was most clearly defined by the cross, and bearing the cross for others was a way to join with Jesus in his word of reconciliation and resurrection.

INWARD REFLECTION

Have you had experiences in your life where suddenly you were in a position to bear the burden of others in a way you might not have chosen for yourself? What was that like?

GODWARD REFLECTION

We've spent a lot of time talking about how we can choose to live with other-centered, co-suffering love. In Simon, however, we have an example of a time when someone didn't get to choose. Simon was pressed into service. Nobody asked him if he was up for it or interested, or even if he was a supporter of Jesus. His burden-bearing served Jesus at that moment but then, in the first generations of the church, it became a point of instruction and encouragement. It is an incredible priviledge to get to choose to serve others; it is much more often the case that circumstances thrust us into a situation where we serve even if we wouldn't have chosen to. Reflect on this and what it might show you about God's work in you and in the world.

PRAYER OF INTENTION

Life may present you with opportunities to carry crosses that do not belong to you.* Write a prayer of intention about who God is inviting you to be in that circumstance.

---

* **Important Note:** Some folks, especially very sensitive folks who grew up in religious communities that emphasized service, might feel a tension between being a good burden-bearer and taking on burdens they shouldn't or really can't. One way to address this tension is to understand that this is one of the purposes of a healthy church community. The other-centered, co-suffering way is a team sport. If I'm in community with you, and I see that you are being "pressed" into service in a way that is unhealthy for you, being co-centered would mean that I notice, and being co-suffering would mean that I help shoulder the burden. That might mean taking the burden on so you didn't need to carry it. It might mean the church teams up to help, like when churches plan a meal train for someone in a crisis. It might mean we become advocates for you in a situation where the battle isn't yours to fight.

DAY 38: DO I MOVE BEYOND THOUGHTS AND PRAYERS?

Luke 23:27-31

REFLECTION

As THE SOLDIERS led Jesus along the streets to the place of execution, crowds began to gather. Among those crowds were women. Perhaps some knew Jesus, or maybe they watched his work and teaching at a distance. Seeing him walk toward his death was too much. They wept. The text says they beat their chests and wailed.

Jesus noticed and gave a grave warning. "Don't weep for me," he said. "Weep for yourselves and your children." Then he said a catastrophe was coming. People would wish they were dead—specifically the children of these women! Jesus' stark words end with the question: "If they do this when the wood is green, what will happen when it is dry?"

They? Who is Jesus referring to? The text is ambiguous. Some commentators think Jesus refers generally to the powerful, perhaps the religious leaders in Jerusalem or agents of Roman power. These are the kind of people who believe their injustice has no consequence. Other commentators think Jesus was prophesying the Roman siege and destruction of Jerusalem that would take place about forty years later.*

For decades, anti-Roman sentiment would foment, driven by violent nationalist factions. Eventually, Rome decided the price of maintaining Judea as a province was too high. Instead of withdrawing and demonstrating weakness to the rest of the Empire, Rome would drop the hammer. The 10th Legion, under the command of General Titus, would lay the city bare, destroying the temple, burning the city to the ground, killing all the defenders and the infirm, and enslaving more than 90,000 people.

In writing a contemporaneous account, Josephus says that after the destruction, witnesses could scarcely believe anyone had ever lived there.† The empire considered this a significant victory and commemorated it in Rome with a grand parade. The Arch of Titus, built to celebrate this event, can still be seen on the Via Sacra in Rome today. The sculptured relief on the arch shows Roman soldiers looting the sacred candlestick and other items from the temple, a warning to any who might oppose the will of the empire. With this violent retribution, Rome would end the ancient nation of Israel.

---

* Brian Zahnd takes this angle on the text, and I found his reading helpful: "Jesus had tried to pull Jerusalem back from its hell-bent ways, but he knew that he had only given Jerusalem a forty-year stay of sentence. Jesus was the green tree who taught and embodied the way of peace and love, yet he was still crucified. The sons of the weeping women of Jerusalem will be the dry wood who will foolishly advocate for the way of war. Jesus is saying that if the Romans can inflict such a fire of suffering on the green tree of peacemaking, what amount of suffering will they kindle in the dry trees of war-waging." Zahnd, Brian. *The Unvarnished Jesus: A Lenten Journey* (p. 144). Kindle Edition.

† You can read Josephus' account. You'll find it in Book 6, Chapters 1-10 of his work, *The War of the Jews*. Here's one source: https://avander.sites.luc.edu/jerusalem/sources/wars6.htm

Jesus was telling the women that crosses were coming for their children. Even if we read this in a spiritualized way, thinking that Jesus is talking about eternal matters, we can't ignore that Jesus was telling these women to be concerned with a genuine and immediate question of destiny. The increasingly incendiary path of violent retribution so many chose would ultimately erupt in a conflagration that would destroy their world. The women of Jerusalem were weeping as they saw injustice and violence inflicted on Jesus. This is a good and human response. When we see injustice right in front of us, it should move us. Our compassion and indignation should arise and move us to respond. We feel the weight of it. Maybe we weep. Maybe we begin to speak up—and sometimes we literally and tritely say, "You're in my thoughts and prayers." This is natural, but it's not enough.

Jesus honored the tears of these women but also challenged them to look beyond him. Injustice is rarely about just one person. It's nearly always the result of a system. In Jesus' case, two systems worked hand in hand: a system of political control enforced by state-sanctioned violence and a system of religious power enforced by moral gatekeeping and corrupt politics. Both of these systems regarded Jesus as a threat.

But all systems of power have a blind spot. The holders of power who depend on these systems always project. The violent see the threat of violence all around them. The politically corrupt believe their opponents are as corrupt as they are. Having been in control for so long, the powerful think they've set the rules of the game. They assume everyone must be playing by the same rules!

This is where they were mistaken. Jesus wasn't a threat because of violence or political corruption. Jesus was a threat because the new kingdom he brought used a different kind of power with different rules. Love has no use for coercion. It does no violence. Truth doesn't play the games of corrupt politicians. As more and more people choose to follow Jesus' way of love and truth,* empires of violence and corruption lose their power. Not only that, but Jesus' way can even set those in power free. Love and truth stand with the oppressed, but they also free the violent and corrupt from the chains of their own system. This is why it's not enough to weep when we see injustice near us. An other-centered compassion should elicit thoughts and prayers in us, but this is only a start. Co-suffering love will impel us into appropriate action, advocacy, and practical care.

Jesus warned the women of Jerusalem that the cross was coming for them and their children. Choosing the way of active love and peacemaking not only helps the person in front of us who is being hurt by injustice, but it will also help others. It will help us; it will help our children. Jesus' way can save us all.

---

* This, it should be noted, is not the same thing as converting to Christianity, joining a church, or filling your time with nice, clean church activities.

INWARD REFLECTION

In the best case, responding to a tragedy by offering "thoughts and prayers" is a short-hand way of expressing shared grief and hope for recovery. In the worst case, it can be a dismissal of the tragedy, a way to perform public grief while ignoring any need to respond with action. Reflect on how you've experienced people's "thoughts and prayers." When has this seemed helpful and supportive? When has it seemed unhelpful?

GODWARD REFLECTION

In today's scripture, Jesus warns about the violent trajectory of his contemporary world. As a thought experiment, imagine God saying something like this to our world today. What warnings do you think God might give today? What actions do you sense God might be inviting us to take?

PRAYER OF INTENTION

This is a difficult topic. Notice where you experience discomfort. Notice if and where your heart sings in response. Write a prayer of intention that emerges from your sense of the Spirit's guidance.

DAY 39: DO I NEED A VIOLENT GOD?

Luke 23:33-38

REFLECTION

ARRIVING at the hill of execution, Jesus was affixed to the crossbeam and then raised into place. Two other crosses were also raised, each bearing a criminal condemned to death. A placard meant to shame and mock was placed above Jesus' head, with the words, "The king of the Jews." The soldiers gambled for Jesus' clothes, a final bit of loot for their trouble. From the cross, Jesus spoke: "Father, forgive them, for they do not know what they are doing."

Standing nearby, you would have heard the soldiers laughing, saying, "If you are special, if you are the King of the Jews, then save yourself!" The religious leaders said something similar, "He saved others; let him save himself . . . if he is the Messiah, God's chosen one." Even one of the criminals crucified next to Jesus echoed these mocking words.

These quips reveal their assumptions.* The Roman soldiers' vision of kingship was built on coercive violence. You got to be king because you could do violence to others while keeping others from doing violence to you. If the soldiers were able to torture and kill you, your status was clear; if you had been a king, you certainly weren't one anymore. The very idea was a joke.

The religious leaders couldn't imagine a Messiah that could be killed. Being chosen by God meant being chosen for blessing, privilege, and power, didn't it? If God allowed someone to threaten the Chosen One, it would only be for one purpose: to bring God glory. How? Those who dared raise a hand against God's anointed would be obliterated or forced to their knees in submission. Someone claiming to be the Messiah who couldn't save themselves from torture and death had proven themselves a liar.

The Roman soldiers and the religious leaders shared the same view of power. Because Jesus was nailed to a cross, he failed to measure up to their definitions. Because he couldn't or wouldn't save himself, because he would not use whatever power he had to defeat his enemies, he wasn't fit to be king or Messiah. Even if he was the Chosen One, he wasn't their Chosen One.

Here, we see something altogether unexpected. On the cross, Jesus looks at those around him — the ones who don't believe in him, the ones who cannot make sense of him because he violated their expectations of power, even the ones actively trying to destroy him — and responds with forgiveness. Not only that, but this forgiveness isn't a transaction. There is no offer of forgiveness in exchange for

---

* Their accusations seem a bitter and sarcastic echo of the temptations Jesus faced in the wilderness.

repentance! Jesus asks the Father to forgive because the people gathered around don't understand the impact of their actions.

The earliest Christians were clear: The cross is a revelation. It teaches us something new about God. God is not out to prove how powerful God is. God has no desire to force us into submission. God's character is, and always has been, other-centered co-suffering love. On the cross, God is human. On the cross, God is weak. On the cross, God tells us what we cannot admit to ourselves: We do not understand; we cannot grasp the full depths of who God is. We've been doing theology for as long as humans could speak. Along the way, we've imagined every shape and size and name for divinity. We've built stunning wonders to honor one deity or another. But even with all the different names, ritual systems, and theological explanations, most have arrived at the same end. God is ultimate power, and that power finally manifests itself in divine violence.

The cross is a multi-faceted revelation. One of the truths it shows, if we are willing to look, is that we are the ones infatuated with violence, retribution, and wrath. We are the ones who will protect our sense of identity with lies and then protect our lies with violence. We are the ones who believe the highest kind of power is the kind that terrifies people into submission. Because we believe this, we project it all onto God. We are the ones who say, "If you don't do what God says, God will torture and kill you." We are the ones who say, "We're right, and if you don't agree with us, you're opposing God." Humans have done this as long as humans have talked and written about God. We've done it in the pages of scripture and in our theological explanations. If our truth leads to abuse and violence, we still feel justified. We've done it so often and for so long, we're certain we're speaking truth.

If the cross reveals the true nature of God, what do we see? When God comes and walks among us, as one of us, what do we notice? In the walk to the cross, God receives our torture and mocking condescension. God takes the brunt of our power fantasies. God receives into God's own self the death we offer as retribution for violating our expectations and power systems. With the cross, God holds all this up like a mirror so that we can truly see ourselves if we are willing to look.

And then, as we see our own blood-soaked hands, willing to kill the ultimate innocent One to protect our ego, God forgives because we don't understand the implications of the path we've inherited and that we choose again and again. Even this is part of the burden God bears with us along the path to reconciliation and new life.*

---

* I understand that this particular understanding of the cross will be challenging for some. Divine violence is built into so many Christian theologies. People often turn to violent images in Revelation, to argue that God will ultimately do violence to those who rebel. Even our core theology of the atonement (what the cross did for humanity) is shot through with expectations that God must do violence to accomplish God's good ends. I understand all of this, and where it comes from. For most of my life, I was in that same theological space. Responding to these questions requires more space than this little book can afford. If you are interested in exploring this idea, and seeing how it has been part of Christian theology, back to the early church, I can recommend the following books: In regard to understanding Revelation and its violent imagery, I recommend Gorman's *Reading Revelation Responsibly: Following the Lamb into the New Creation*. In regard to understanding the Atonement, and ideas about God's violence toward the Son, I recommend Jersak's *A More Christlike God: A More Beautiful Gospel*. In regard to handling other passages of violence in scripture, I also recommend Jersak's *A More Christlike Word: Reading Scripture the Emmaus Way*. All three of these books are accessible to most readers, and all provide ample access to sources for further study.

INWARD REFLECTION

Take a moment to consider if you need God to be violent, and, if so, why? If your immediate answer is "because the Bible says so" or is rooted in theological explanations that are important to you, take a moment to think beyond that. Consider on an emotional and spiritual basis why it might seem indispensable to you that God is violent. If that's not your picture of God, it might serve you to take a moment to consider, with compassion and good faith, why, for some people, it feels critical, even comforting, to believe that God is violent.

GODWARD REFLECTION

What does this passage show you about the nature of God? What might this mean in terms of your relationship with God? What might it mean in terms of how you relate to others?

PRAYER OF INTENTION

Considering what you sense this passage tells you about God, write a prayer of intention in response.

DAY 40: DO I THINK THE CROSS WAS JUST FOR ME?

Luke 23:39-43

REFLECTION

ONE OF THE classic Christian images is a silhouette of three crosses on a hilltop. Our theology often leads us to focus on only one. That's the one that matters, right? Our eyes are on Jesus' sacrifice. That's fine, but momentarily, zoom out and hold all three crosses in your mind.

For the Roman soldiers tasked with this bloody work, the day Jesus was crucified was just another day.* For them, his crucifixion wasn't remarkable. I know this isn't easy to conceive. Two thousand years of Christian imagery has formed our spiritual imaginations. For most, the cross immediately brings Jesus to mind and whatever theological

---

* This is another spot where Brian Zahnd's reading of this text pierced me. While I've known about the others crucified along with Jesus, I had never seriously considered their presence in the gospel as a statement of God's solidarity with humanity.

explanations you've been taught, but that's a trick of retrospection. Without the recollection of Jesus' first followers, later recorded in the Gospels and Paul's letters, this event would be lost to history. By itself, Jesus' crucifixion wasn't especially memorable. It wasn't even the only one that day. This was a batch job, three more to add to the tally of thousands crucified over the years and across the empire.

Hold all three crosses in mind. There is gospel truth even here. At this moment of suffering, Jesus is not alone. He is with others who are suffering. He is to be found among the condemned. He is a member of the great extended family of those who are little more than a sad curiosity to passers-by or even a parental warning. "Keep your nose clean. You don't want to end up like that poor guy over there." He is one of the many roughly handled, afforded no dignity or respect because they "had it coming to them." He is among the company of the lynched.*

On Golgotha, Jesus is one of three. Those three are only that day's roster out of thousands crucified. All those crucified by Rome are just a fraction of the countless shamed, tortured, and killed at the effect of powers beyond their control. Jesus dies on the cross, flanked by men society would rather kill than deal with. This happens so often, and in so many ways, it's now just part of the background buzz of civilization.

I know our minds flinch, immediately gilding the scene with atonement theology. We turn this event into the final

---

* This is stark language that causes discomfort for some. If you feel that, take notice of it. The discomfort points to something important. If you'd like to look further into the connections between Jesus' crucifixion and the heritage of lynching, I recommend you read Dr. James Cone's book, *The Cross and the Lynching Tree*. It is one of the most important and influential works of theology written in the modern era.

puzzle piece that completes the picture of our salvation story. Before we turn away from the horrific scene, notice what our minds don't want to accept. We say that Jesus walked among and welcomed outcasts. But notice. He doesn't just walk among them. He becomes one of them, not in some symbolic way, but quite literally. He suffers with them. He experiences degradation with them. He is treated as less than human with them. He dies with them. Even this is part of the Incarnation. Shouldn't this challenge our theology and, thus, our practice?

What changes if, at least for a moment, we see Jesus as just one of three that day? If we hold that Jesus is God, what would that mean for him to be just one of the three executed on that hill? Maybe it means that God knows from personal experience the excruciating pain of powerlessness and humiliation. If this is true, it upends our understanding of the Divine. God knows what it feels like to be fully in the power of someone who counts you as nothing, who hurts you and degrades you, even while saying they are doing it for a good reason.

The collective intuition of human religion frequently has landed on the assumption that only a powerful deity, unable to be touched by suffering, can help us. When we are powerful, when we get our way, that's when we imagine we are somehow feeling the most like God. Jesus turns this upside down. Even in the darkest places of pain, God is present. Even in our most isolating, humiliating experiences, God is with us. This is deeply comforting, but it also unbolts a door of consciousness we may not want opened. If God is with us in our painful powerlessness, then surely God is with the others. All the others. The ones we would rather not look in the eye. The ones we dismiss as the inevitable casualties of maintaining a society that is comfortable for us. The ones we think had it coming. The ones that power crushes.

Walking Jesus' path will lead us into solidarity with those our society would rather kill than deal with. It's one thing to see the cross as God's tragic sacrifice to benefit me eternally. It's an entirely different thing to see the cross as God standing with all of humanity and inviting us to do the same.

INWARD REFLECTION

Different theological traditions have offered various explanations for the meaning of the crucifixion. Western Christian theology often focuses on the impact on an individual and their eternal salvation. In today's entry, I invite you to set aside this individualistic reading and imagine what it might mean for all of us collectively. What does salvation mean to you if it is not just about you but about all of us — especially those most hard-pressed?

GODWARD REFLECTION

The author of the New Testament book of Hebrews made this radical claim: Jesus is "the reflection of God's glory and the exact imprint of God's very being."* If this is so, what might the circumstances of Jesus' crucifixion between two thieves tell us about God's nature?

PRAYER OF INTENTION

If Jesus' cross is an example of God standing with all humanity, even the most despised, that says something about what it means to follow in Jesus' steps. Write a prayer of intention that emerges from your reflection on this.

---

* Hebrews 1:3.

CODA: CAN I LEAVE THE FEAR OF DEATH BEHIND?

John 19:38-42

REFLECTION

IN THESE FEW LINES, we are shown a scene both tender and terrible. With most of Jesus' friends scattered, Joseph of Arimathea and Nicodemus took it upon themselves to care for Jesus' body. They removed him from the cross, quickly prepared his body for burial, and carried him to a nearby empty tomb. A tender act of love and respect; the painful acknowledgment that Jesus is dead. This was a moment of profound grief.

In your mind's eye, watch Joseph and Nicodemus, having finished their work, duck out of the tomb and silently roll the stone into place. Hear the grating stone roll into the groove carved for it and the leaden thud as it drops into place. The implacable force of the Roman Empire had done what it always did, plowing over any resistance. The inertia of corrupt leadership held out one more time. These two men were not just sealing the tomb against robbers and scavengers; they were (at least in their minds, at that moment) closing the door on the story of Jesus. The hopes and fears of all the years met, and fear and violence won out.

Looking back from the vantage of two thousand years of Easters, we naturally want to rush to the good part. God brings forth life from the tomb! Christ defeats death by death. We are raised to the newness of life along with him! If we hold the image of Jesus crucified in mind for long, it's often so we can see past the horror to the shining nobility, the highest act of love.* From there, it's a short transition to seeing Jesus emerge from the tomb in a halo of glory, death conquered. But there is value in pausing in the liminal space between the cross and the resurrection.

Christians believe that in Jesus, God came to walk among us. We call this the Incarnation. Holy Saturday† may be the

---

* There certainly are many Christian traditions that focus on Jesus' suffering on the cross. Historically, this seems to wax and wane in emphasis, apparently peaking in times and places when people are trying to make sense of significant suffering. For example, in Western Europe, there was a marked increase in hymns and Christian art that focused on Jesus' suffering during and in the immediate aftermath of the Black Plague. Since the Reformation, and particularly in places where people are more comfortable, Jesus' suffering on the cross seems to shift its meaning. In these places, the theological emphasis moves away from identification with suffering and focuses more on the cross as a necessary step in the process of atonement. In the first case, Jesus suffers with us, identifying with suffering humanity. This also provides a sacred focus for those who suffer, enabling them to see their suffering as participating in the life of Christ. In the second case, Jesus suffers for us, primarily as part of his sacrifice, which accomplishes salvation. These two themes are present in Christian theology at nearly all historical points, and both have scriptural warrant, but it seems to be the case that in different historical contexts, one or the other becomes more central, or in some cases, is presented as the only accurate interpretation. For the purposes of this book, with its focus on personal attitude and outlook, I've focused on the aspect of identification rather than the aspect of atonement.

† If, like me, you were raised in a Protestant or non-liturgical church

single most transgressive part of the Incarnation, with the capacity to change entirely how we relate to our life and death. Why? The book of Hebrews tells us that Jesus experienced every temptation and experience common to humanity.* We often talk about the wonder of God entering into our mess, walking in our shoes. Well, the one experience that binds all of humanity together is death. We all die, rich and poor, every color, every gender, all of us, no matter how much we fight it. Death is our universal inheritance and fate. Unexpected tragedy strikes. Sometimes, others do violence to us. Always, our bodies eventually fail, refusing to do what we ask of them. One way or another, usually against our will, we die.

Perhaps Nietzsche thought he was being scandalous when he declared God's death, but his words shouldn't offend any Christian who knows their own story. At the heart of our faith is this mystery: God didn't just cosplay humanity. God became human. Totally. Completely. Breaking every expectation we have for deity, God died.

In the late fourth century, the church was sorting out how to explain the paradox of Jesus having both a human and Divine nature and what this meant for salvation.† Describing

---

tradition, you might not know the names given to the days of the Passion week. Palm Sunday is the Sunday prior to Easter, commemorating Jesus' triumphal entry into Jerusalem. Maundy Thursday is the day that Jesus met in the Upper Room with the disciples. (Maundy comes from the Latin word for Mandate, referring to Jesus' new commandment, given in the Upper Room discourse.) Good Friday is the day of the crucifixion. This is followed by Holy Saturday, the day Jesus spent in the tomb. Which, of course, leads to Resurrection Sunday, also called Easter.

* Hebrews 4:15.
† This is a long and complex conversation better suited to historical theology texts. In short, the question was how Jesus could be both Divine and human. Did Jesus have a fully human body, mind, and will? If so, when did his Divine nature come into play? Did he simultaneously have two wills,

how God in Jesus took on the entirety of the human condition, Gregory of Nazianzus wrote: "That which is not assumed is not healed. That which is united to God will be saved."* Well, one of the human things assumed by Christ is death.

The ancient church consistently taught that Christ entered into death, defeated it from the inside, and that this provided immediate benefit for humanity. Be clear: They did not primarily mean that one day, in a distant future, you would live a life beyond death. They did believe that, but they also believed that right now, in the present moment, the power of death had been defeated. They saw death as a kind of corruption that drove humanity to anxiety, fear, and sin. Because Christ took on our death, death is no longer our master. These early Christian theologians took the Apostle Paul literally when he said that nothing, not even death, can separate us from the love of God.†

We know Jesus' resurrection did not end the phenomenon of death — people still die — but by assuming human death, death itself is redeemed and made sacred. Like birth and

---

one human, one Divine? Or did Jesus have a fully Divine nature and only appear to be human? There were significant arguments over this. Arguably, the Nicene Creed was written entirely to put an end to this debate. The solution that won the day and became orthodox Christian teaching was to maintain the paradox rather than try to parse the mechanics for a single solution.

* St. Gregory of Nazianzus' Letter to Cledonius, written in the late 4th century. This letter was a theological discussion of the nature of Christ, as part of an argument against certain teachers who were claiming that Jesus did not have a fully human mind. Summarizing the teachings of the early Church Fathers, Gregory made the point that Jesus was fully and entirely human, and that this alone is what made the salvation of humanity possible. Essentially, Gregory claimed, any part of human experience not found in Jesus was not redeemed.

† Romans 8:38-39.

baptism, it is now one more thing we do, following the example of Jesus. He died with us; we die with him.* The early church taught that death defanged is death no longer feared. Instead of a haunting spirit, it has become a sacrament, a sacred rest that all humanity shares with God. In Christ, we live and breathe and have our being.† In him, we also have our death.

Christians celebrate rising with Christ, and rightly so. But we must also talk about Saturday in the tomb. I think the intuition of the Patristic theologians was correct: In so many ways, our fear of death corrupts our lives. We run and work and fill every waking moment with distraction so we don't have to face the idea of our demise. We idolize adolescent bodies and spend our time and resources trying in vain to hold back the effects of time. Not only that, but we cannot look certain people in the eye — those with chronic pain, those living with cancer or AIDS, the very old, and many others — because their very existence reminds us that our bodies, too, will fail.

Even our desperate attempts to deny the structural inequality in our society are manifestations of our fear of death. We tell stories that suggest people without homes, healthcare, or enough money to afford leisure time are only

---

* Hans Urs von Balthasar, a modern Catholic theologian puts it this way: "Jesus was truly dead, because he really became a man as we are, a son of Adam, and therefore, despite what one can sometimes read in certain theological works, he did not use the so-called brief time of his death for manner of 'activities' in the world beyond. In the same way that, upon earth, he was in solidarity with the living, so, in the tomb, he is in solidarity with the dead . . . Each human being lies in his own tomb. And with this condition Jesus is in complete solidarity." Oakes, S.J., Edward T. "'He Descended into Hell': The Depths of God's Self-Emptying Love on Holy Saturday in the Thought of Hans Urs von Balthasar." *In Exploring Kenotic Christology: The Self-Emptying of God*, 218–45, 2010. 236.

† Acts 17:28.

experiencing the consequences of their choices, failures, or moral flaws. Why? Because those stories allow us to believe that we could stop these terrible things from happening to us because we are different—wiser, more prepared, and more righteous. We would rather not contemplate our powerlessness to stop these things happening, in the very same way that we are ultimately powerless to prevent death.

But Jesus' Saturday in the tomb tells us that even death is sacred now. There truly is no experience we can have outside the reach of God's understanding or presence. And if, in death, we are not alone but are held in Christ, then there is nothing to fear. If there is nothing to fear, then there is no reason not to love. Freed from the haunting fear of death, we can throw ourselves into a life of generous, other-centered, co-suffering love.

And so we finally come, at last, to the resurrection. For what is new life if it is not the power to live without fear of death? Can we claim to be people of the resurrection if we love frugally or are meticulous and miserly in service? When we act in fear of judgment or exclusion, are we animated by the resurrection? When we decide that, above all else, we must protect our own skin (or comfort), which side of the tomb's stone doorway are we on?

Most Christians hold that there is life after death and that the main point of resurrection is that, in some way, we will live eternally in the presence of God. As good of news as that may be, it is also news about another day, likely distant and surely abstract. In contrast to this mindset, early Christian preachers and theologians were remarkably focused on understanding the resurrection as a present experience. Athanasius, one of the most influential early Christian thinkers, wrote: "But since the Savior's raising the body, no longer is death fearsome, but all believers in Christ tread on it as nothing, and would rather choose to die than deny their faith in Christ."*

In his death and resurrection, Jesus broke the curse of death and corruption. What remains? To live. To live as Christ. To pour ourselves out in loving service. To participate in God's gentle, gracious work of reconciliation and restoration. And to do so, no longer driven by fear of death, but rather because every moment that remains for us is a new opportunity to follow Jesus' way.

"A new command I give you," Jesus said. "That you love one another. Just as I have loved you, you also should love one another."† This command was never about proving belonging, earning salvation, or obligatory acts of service. It was always meant to define the way forward.

So it remains.

---

* Athanasius. *On the Incarnation*. Translated by John Behr. Yonkers, NY: St Vladimir's Seminary Press, 2011. 27.
† John 13:34, NRSVue.

INWARD REFLECTION

In what ways does fear of death, and its lesser manifestations of fear of pain and insecurity, influence your life and decision-making?

GODWARD REFLECTION

Consider the meaning of Holy Saturday for your understanding of God's nature. What does it mean to you that God experienced death and, in doing so, made death sacred? How can this shape both your own feelings about death as well as your feelings about life?

CLOSING PRAYER OF INTENTION

As you close today's reflection and your time with this book, consider the forty previous prayers of intention you've written. You may even want to take a few minutes to review them. In light of what you've experienced here, write a concluding prayer of intention about who you believe God is inviting you to be.

APPENDIX 1: WHY 40 DAYS? WHY LENT?

WHY 40 DAYS?

THIS BOOK WAS DESIGNED to guide you through forty days of spiritual focus, reflecting on Jesus' mindset and interactions. Why take six weeks to focus on a particular theme? That question is worth answering.

We live in a world where industrialization and market-driven techno-capitalism promise that our every need can be met just in time — if we can pay. The grocery store has tomatoes year round (even though most of the year, those tomatoes lack the qualities essential to a good tomato experience). A new computer or a set of plastic wall hooks can arrive in our driveway tomorrow (never mind that the delivery driver is penalized for taking bathroom breaks). That's the spirit of the age: We want what we want when we want it, and that's always now.

This seismic shift has changed many things about society and human experience. One of those changes worth noticing is how many of us are losing touch with seasons. For most of human history, we've learned how life works from watching the natural world. There are seasons for rest and for growth. There are seasons for productivity and seasons for recovery. The seasons last for a while, but, always, they give way to the next season. Even though our culture is desperate to defy these seasons with air conditioners, climate-controlled vehicles, and fresh fruit flown from around the world, the seasons pass.

There is wisdom that comes from paying attention to the natural course of seasons. It's a wisdom familiar to farmers and others who work outside. It's a wisdom pre-industrialized cultures paid attention to. Try to plant in winter or harvest in spring, and your efforts will be wasted. Winter might feel long, but it's not forever. Each season is productive in a different way. Winter's rest is just as important as spring's planting or fall's harvest.

Many of us raised in Christian spaces were taught the importance of a daily devotional practice. In some circles, our consistency with this "quiet time" was almost a measure of our faith. We might have been taught specific modes of prayer and Bible study. Some of us were taught to journal in particular ways. Spiritual practices like these can be profoundly formational and grounding, but for many of us, this training came with an expectation of dedication. Dedication was measured by how often we kept our practice (every day?) and how long (oh, an hour at least!). We were over-awed by the example of faith heroes like Martin Luther, who is purported to have once said, "I have so much to do that I shall spend the first three hours in prayer." OK, Martin.

In many faith communities, there was little to no concern for mental health or acknowledgment of how various temperaments and learning styles might experience these practices differently. There was rarely any awareness that spiritual focus naturally waxes and wanes, and there was no understanding that the waning wasn't faithlessness. After all, a farmer who doesn't get up early to plant during winter isn't a lousy farmer. They are simply living in alignment with the seasons.

The spiritual life can't be run like a factory or a barracks. Entrepreneurial hustle won't generate spiritual growth. A healthy inner life will have seasons. There will be times of intense focus and learning. Those seasons must be followed by times of rest and reflection. That's when the deep inner work below our conscious awareness takes place. This isn't something to fear or be ashamed of. It's not evidence of a lack of dedication. It's how life works.

The ancient Hebrew manuscript Ecclesiastes held that paying attention to the seasons was a spiritual essential.

> For everything there is a season and a time for every matter under heaven . . . a time to plant and a time to pluck up what is planted . . . a time to break down and a time to build up.*

In our warp-speed culture, committing to a particular spiritual focus for forty days is an act of resistance. This forty-day period appears in scripture in several places. Famously, Moses communed with God on Mt. Sinai, and Jesus resisted temptation in the wilderness for forty days. This is a window of focus long enough to shift your behavior and thinking, but it's also not unending. It's an opportunity to stick with something for a season, even when it doesn't offer an immediate payoff. At the same time, it's a manageable period of focus that will come to an end. That ending creates space for reflection, rest, and the natural breathing-in-breathing-

---

* Ecclesiastes 3:1-8, NRSVue.

out of spiritual growth. Don't rush into the next thing. (Even during the forty days! If you need to sit with the ideas in a certain day's entry for a few days, that's OK, too.) Rest. Reflect. Ruminate. Let the seeds planted in your time of intensity germinate, and watch how they flower.

WHY LENT IN PARTICULAR?

You can, of course, use this book any time you like. There is, however, a specific period in the year when many Christians will be sharing the same seasonal focus. That season is called Lent. To be clear, this book is not about Lent, and you don't need to observe Lent to use this book. But because this book is about taking a directed season of introspection for your spiritual health, Lent is a great match. And, if you grew up in a non-liturgical church like I did, you might not know about this meaningful resource available to you. So, skip this section if it does not apply or isn't interesting to you.

I came late to Lent. The church I grew up in didn't observe it (Lent was too Catholic for us). All I knew about Lent was that a couple of my friends got ashy smudges on their foreheads that they wore for a day or two and that some people tried hard to "give something up for Lent." If you're like me and didn't grow up with Lent, it's worth taking a moment to talk about what it is and how it might benefit you.

Lent is presently a 40-day fast that leads up to Easter. Most Christian denominations observe it. It wasn't always a 40-day fast, but it's always been a fast that leads up to the celebration of the Resurrection.* Because the date for Easter

---

* I say most because that's true! The only Christian groups that don't observe Lent are some Protestant churches on the Evangelical and Charismatic end of the pool. Lent is practiced by the Catholic Church, the

shifts annually,* the beginning of Lent also shifts. It starts with Ash Wednesday, which is usually sometime in February.† Lent is quite ancient. Evidence shows that by the end of the second century CE, most Christian churches were celebrating *Pascha*,‡ or the Feast of the Resurrection.§

Of course, Christians didn't invent fasting. In most ancient cultures, fasting was a way to prepare the body and spirit for something significant, like a coming-of-age ceremony, a spiritual journey, or taking certain vows. Fasting was a regular practice in Judaism, and since almost all the first Christians were Jewish, it makes sense that this practice would find its way into Christianity. Catechumens (people preparing to be baptized into Christianity) would fast prior to baptism. The earliest churches baptized new believers every Easter, which meant there was a baptismal fasting period that

---

Episcopal church, the Anglican Church, all the Christian Orthodox communions, as well as most Lutheran and Methodist churches.

* Weird, right? The date for Easter, as celebrated in the Western Church (pretty much all of Christianity that isn't Eastern Orthodox), was set at the Council of Nicaea in 325 CE. That date? The first Sunday which follows the new full moon on or immediately following the vernal equinox. So, you know — just like how we schedule stuff today.

† Ash Wednesday is forty-six days before Easter Sunday. Why forty six? Because Lent is a fast, and since every Sunday is a celebration of the resurrection, there is no obligation to fast on Sunday. So, to get a 40-day fast, you need six extra days to account for Sundays. The earliest Ash Wednesday can be is February 4th. The latest is March 10th.

‡ The word in Greek is πασχα, pronounced *pascha* or *pah-skuh*.

§ For example, in his church history (written in the 4th century CE) Eusebius relates a letter from Irenaeus to Pope Victor. This letter, which would have been written in the late 2nd century, detailed the arguments between various groups as to the exact and proper dating of the passion and resurrection and how to celebrate it. It's interesting to note that Irenaeus supports his own views attributing them to his ancestors. If that's true, it puts the celebration of Easter within a generation or two of the resurrection. (Schaff and Wace, *Eusebius: Church History, Life of Constantine the Great, and Oration in Praise of Constantine*. Vol. 1., Book V, Chapter 24)

coincidentally led up to Easter. By the 4th century, this preparatory fast extended to the whole church, not just those preparing for baptism, although the exact form and length of the fast varied from place to place. At the end of the sixth century, Pope Gregory I standardized Lent in the form, date, and length that it still exists today.

Modern people, who live in a world of historic abundance, tend to think of fasts primarily as intentional deprivation, but in the ancient world, where most were poor and always had less than they needed, this was not the case. A religious fast was primarily a period of focus and purification. It was a time for intentional repentance, reparation, and renewal of spiritual commitment. From that ancient intent, Christians who observe Lent are encouraged to commit to a period of increased spiritual practice. That might include giving up certain things as a means of increasing attention to spiritual things. It might mean setting aside certain obligations and opening more time to devote to spiritual practice. It might include an intentional period of reconciliation, seeking to make things right with others. It often also consists of an increased focus on spiritual practices like daily scripture reading and meditation, prayers, and other practices that focus on the interior life.

There is a tendency, especially among those of us who've grown up in legalistic religion, to see these things as obligations and spiritual performance. If that's your background (as it is mine), it's important to note that none of this is meant to gain credit or approval from God. We are already profoundly loved and accepted. Spiritual practices don't force growth to happen. Growth is the work of the Spirit that happens according to the timeline of the Spirit. But practices like these can be a part of our training in maturity, helping us to practice being present to God. The added bonus of Lent is that when you participate, you join countless Christians worldwide and across time who have found this season of introspection and spiritual focus meaningful.

AUTHOR'S GRATITUDE

Thanks so much for spending this time with me. Your time is the most valuable thing you have, and it's an enormous honor that you've spent some of yours with this book.

If you've found this helpful, I'd love to hear from you. Everything I write and do online can be found by going to my website www.MarcAlanSchelske.com. I write about practical spiritual growth in the realm that lies beyond the constricting influence of fundamentalism. You can find me on many social media sites either as @Schelske or as @MarcAlanSchelske. You can also email me at Marc@MarcAlanSchelske.com. If you take the time to email, and you're kind about it, I'll respond.

Remember, in this one present moment, you are loved, you are known, and you are not alone.

MORE FROM MARC

APPRENTICESHIP NOTES NEWSLETTER

THE BEST WAY TO stay connected with Marc is to subscribe to his monthly-ish newsletter. *Apprenticeship Notes* includes an essay not published elsewhere, insider commentary on Marc's writing and podcast, as well as recommended books and spiritual practices. No spam.

Opt in at www.MarcOptIn.com.

JOURNALING FOR SPIRITUAL GROWTH

Over the centuries, journaling has emerged as one of the most consistently transformative practices, recommended by leaders across spiritual traditions, therapists, coaches, and others. In six weeks, learn a flexible and graceful journaling practice with guidance to build a sustainable habit that will serve you for years to come. Available in paperback and eBook.

www.journalingforspiritualgrowth.com

THE WISDOM OF YOUR HEART

Are you listening to the wisdom of your heart? Your emotions are trying to tell you something. Learning to listen to the truth revealed in our emotions is not only important for a well-lived life but also vital for spiritual growth. Available in paperback, eBook, and audiobook read by the author.
    www.thewisdomofyourheart.com

UNTANGLE WORKBOOK

Emotions don't have to be confusing. They are messages from our deepest places, and they bring with them important understanding if we can learn how to listen. When we learn this skill, our emotions can become a resource for wisdom to help us navigate life and relationships well. Lay-flat ring-bound journal with prompts for systematically processing emotional experiences. Available on Amazon and at:
    www.untangleworkbook.com

THE UNTANGLED HEART WORKSHOP

Trauma therapist Byron Kehler M.S., and Marc Alan Schelske present this on-demand five-hour online training that addresses the role emotions play in a healthy life, what is happening in the brain and body when we feel emotions, and a simple-to-understand roadmap for experiencing and understanding those emotions.
    www.untangledheartcourse.com

DISCOVER YOUR AUTHENTIC CORE VALUES

Other people's agendas are competing for your time and resources. You use a schedule and a budget so that your time and money are used intentionally. Without those tools, your decisions would be pulled in every direction by other people's wants and needs. Identifying your core values will help you stop living in reactivity. *Discovering Your Authentic Core Values* walks you step-by-step through a simple process that will help you name what is truly most important to you. Available on Amazon and at:

www.AuthenticCoreValues.com

NOT JUST ONE MORE THING: SPIRITUAL GROWTH FOR BUSY PEOPLE

Is it possible to grow spiritually in the midst of a busy life? You want to grow, but your life is full and fast-paced. You want to slow down, but you're not sure how. Making ends meet, raising kids, taking care of the lawn, moving forward in your career — these things all take time and energy, and you can't opt out of most of them. This ten-week online course can help you find a way forward toward a life that is more than just keeping your spiritual head above water. The course is designed to fit into an already busy life, and it will help you make tangible changes quickly.

www.live210.com/busy-growth

www.ingramcontent.com/pod-product-compliance
Lightning Source LLC
Chambersburg PA
CBHW032035290426
44110CB00012B/807